ESSENTIAL
FORD CAPRI

ESSENTIAL
FORD CAPRI

THE CARS AND THEIR STORY 1969-87

CHRIS REES

BAY VIEW
BOOKS

Published 1997 by Bay View Books Ltd
The Red House, 25-26 Bridgeland Street,
Bideford, Devon EX39 2PZ, UK

Edited by Mark Hughes
Typesetting and design by Chris Fayers & Sarah Ward

ISBN 1 901432 01 7
Printed in Spain

CONTENTS

FORD'S PERSONAL COUPE INHERITANCE

Any investigation of the origins of the Capri inevitably ends up in America, since all roads lead to Lee Iacocca, the charmed Ford executive. It was he who effectively invented the so-called 'personal coupe', of which the Capri was the first European embodiment. Iacocca was the father of the Capri's direct ancestor, the Ford Mustang.

Undoubted genius created the Mustang in what was perhaps the greatest marketing coup ever. Nothing in the Mustang was very new technically speaking – indeed, it was a rather archaic machine and certainly no sports car – but it made more people say 'I have to have one' than any other car in history. The Mustang was an all-star new car and an unbelievable frenzy surrounded its launch. It took less than two years to sell a million, a world record that stood for over 20 years. That set the seal on a whole new type of car, and within two years the rest of Detroit had to have a 'ponycar' competitor.

The car which gave the Capri birth was Ford's spectacularly successful 'personal coupe', the Mustang. Not only its concept but many of its design details were transplanted into Europe's own 'ponycar'.

What the Mustang possessed was Texan hatfuls of irresistible style, near-infinite flexibility of options, all the practicality of a saloon, and cheap, cheap prices. Ford reasoned that such a winning formula would surely have appeal in Europe as well as America, and so in November 1964 it instituted a project for a new European 'personal coupé'. Project Colt was born.

The notion of Ford-badged coupés had already been tried several times in Europe. Their starting points were decidedly unlike that of the future Capri, which was conceived (like the Mustang) as a model in its own right. Ford's previous attempts at coupés were almost always mere metalwork jobs on existing saloons.

Although the Capri name first appeared in 1952 on a Lincoln, the 1961 Ford Consul Capri saw its first use in Britain. This 'proto-Capri' was merely a two-door version of the Consul Classic, and certainly *not* a popular personal coupé.

The end results were never particularly successful.

In Britain, the first Ford coupé was a Capri – the 1961 Consul Capri. This peculiar exercise in style over content is now almost forgotten, remaining notable only for its name. It was the precursor of the eponymous subject of this book, although, in fact, the first instance of the Capri name being used was on a 1952 Lincoln.

The '61 Consul Capri was not a carefully thought-out 'personal coupé' but merely a two-door version of the Consul Classic 315. The styling was distinctly trans-Atlantic in flavour, with tail fins, sculpted wing lines and 'cowhorn' rear bumpers. Somehow it looked gauche and suffered as the relation of the Consul Classic, the closest Ford has come to producing a lemon. The Consul Classic has the unenviable distinction of having had the shortest production life of any British Ford, lasting only from 1961 to '63, because it had no place in Ford's line-up following the launch of the Cortina in 1962. The Consul Capri, however, lasted an extra year, but its existence was always highly marginal: only 18,716 were made in its ephemeral three-year life span.

In Germany, the Taunus occupied a position roughly equivalent to the Consul and Cortina. Ford of Germany produced a two-door coupé version of the Taunus 12M P4 from 1963, but it was little more than a saloon with a different roof, and it certainly had none of the desirability of a personal coupé. The same can be said of the coupé version of the larger Taunus 20M, offered from 1964.

More interesting was the coupé that Italian coachbuilder OSI built on the basis of the German Taunus 20M. Ford sold this unusual car through its own dealerships on the continent in 1967-68. But this was definitely not a production Ford, being hand-built, highly specialised and very expensive, costing almost twice as much as a 20M saloon. Only 2000 were made before OSI went bust in '68.

None of these coupé precursors had the appeal of what would become the Capri, and by comparison they were extremely poor sellers. Unlike the Capri, they were not designed from the ground up as a unique and distinct model, and they certainly did not share the Capri's Mustang-style magic formula: cheap prices, a huge spread of tailor-made options, a sports/family split personality that made the best of both worlds, and a shape that was destined to become a classic.

No, the inspiration for the Capri was American through and through. That is not to say that it merely copied a successful formula. The idea – and even the original design – came from Dearborn, but Ford's European wing developed the model from a distinctly European engineering perspective to suit European tastes. The fact that the production Capri was so popular in the US, as well as across Europe, confirms that the concept was fundamentally right, and had truly universal appeal. It was the definitive European Ponycar.

Italian coachbuilder OSI made this coupé in series in 1967 for Ford on a German Taunus 20M floorpan. Unlike the Capri, it was expensive, hand-built, very rare and rather compromised in its shape.

Birth of the Car You Always Promised Yourself

The blazing success of the Mustang made a European equivalent logically imperative and potentially very lucrative. Although European buyers were not as affluent as their American counterparts, the trend was certainly in the same direction: it would be only a matter of time before American inspired 'lifestyle' cars achieved similar popularity.

As such, Ford wanted to be at the forefront of any future 'personal car' revolution in Europe, just as it was proving to be with the Mustang in the 'States. The 'Stang arrived in April 1964 and was so overwhelmingly successful that Ford HQ in Dearborn had little hesitation in approving a similar concept for Europe within months of the Mustang going on sale. Project Colt received the green light in November 1964, the Colt name paying homage to the ponycar that inspired it.

At that stage, Ford's image in Europe as a company that was becoming increasingly motor sport oriented was

The first styling proposals came from studios in America, Germany and Britain. This is a rather wild American effort.

also persuasive. The Anglia had become the favourite of privateers and tuners, and had finished second in the 1963 East African Safari. The Lotus Cortina had gone one better, winning the 1964 Safari in convincing style. The German Ford competitions department took longer to get going, but the best intentions were certainly present. A sporting mass-market Ford made considerable marketing sense.

In Dearborn, Ford's management could hardly have been more confident about the new car. The parameters for the Colt were firm, echoing the strong features of the Mustang: sporty looks, seating for four, low prices, a wide choice of engines and equipment, and a sporting flavour in action. In other words, the Capri had to look and feel

Mock-ups were built in 1965-66 for clinic reaction. Two examples show strange side accent (top) and a significant Mustang element (above).

like a sports car but have much of the family practicality of a saloon, and be affordable into the bargain.

There was one further logistical requirement: the new car had to use as many components as possible from existing Ford models to keep costs down. That meant, for instance, no new engines. So just as the Mustang had been based on the compact Falcon, so the Colt would initially be based on the still-fresh Cortina, which had been launched in 1962.

The brief was duly issued in early 1965 to the three main studios in Ford's global empire: America, Britain and Germany. Each came up with its own styling models, but one of the American submissions eventually prevailed. The design was 'clinicked' in various cities across Europe

during 1965, the public being asked to give their opinions on the newcomer in closed viewings without being told who the maker was. The reaction was positive and Ford proceeded.

A number of refined styling proposals followed and, by late 1965, the idea of the 'hockey stick' body side accent was already in place. In July 1966, the go-ahead was given in principle to develop Colt as a production model, although the formal approval required to get the car into production did not in fact arrive until a year later at a meeting chaired by Henry Ford II. The plan was to launch the new car in the autumn of 1968, although that date would prove a little optimistic. Some £20 million was assigned by Ford of Britain as a development budget.

Working prototypes were built during the latter half of 1966, initially by a team of British engineers based at the then-new Dunton facility. The team was headed by John Hitchman, the man who had previously been

The 1966 mock-up that would go on to be developed further. Note the 'hockey-stick' side accent and dummy louvres behind the doors, features which would persist in the production Capri. Technicians built up a full-sized Colt prototype in glass-fibre early in 1966.

responsible for the development engineering on the Consul Capri.

Those initial studies were simply rebodied Cortinas with modified suspension to cope with the reduced weight. They were based around engines ranging from the 1.3-litre in-line 'four' up to the 2.0-litre Corsair V4; at that time, anything larger was not yet in the picture, although the big 'Essex' 3.0-litre V6 would later be earmarked for the Capri. Eventually, the Cortina basis would be eased out, and a unique floorpan would be developed, albeit with a wheelbase all but identical to the Cortina's. Both front and rear tracks were also wider.

Testing began at Boreham in Essex, although the project extended, as Ford of Europe was formed, to become more Europe-wide. Ford of Germany became more closely involved, and developed its own programme based around the quite different range of engines it was then producing. Much of the road testing, for both British and German cars, was done on Belgian roads.

Various working prototypes were constructed with badges reading GBX or Flowline. Most of the features which would become familiar on the Capri had already been set: the hockey-stick side sculptures, fastback roof

line, dummy air louvres in front of the rear wheels, narrow front grille, and so on. But there remained one significant difference from the finished version: the rear three-quarter windows, which had been designed with an angular shape. It quickly became apparent at customer clinics that there were significant objections to this design. Rear seat passengers – already pushed for space – felt claustrophobic because of the large area of metal surrounding them. In response, Ford's designers tried to extend the square window rearwards but this did little to improve matters. In the end, their solution was the classic C-bend rear window shape, and this finally seemed to alleviate the complaints. With the body shape finalised, formal signing-off occurred in October 1967.

So far, the project had always been referred to as 'Colt'

Colt styling proposal (above) at Olympia in 1966, part of Ford's ongoing market research. Members of the public were invited to make their views felt about the new car. To disguise its origins, this car was badged GBX. Note the tucked-in flying rear buttresses. After the clinics, the shape of the Capri was refined again and here (right) it is virtually finalised, although the rear window is still a squared-off shape. There was constant complaint about claustrophobia in the rear passenger area.

but researches indicated that Mitsubishi had already used the name on a car launched in 1963. The search for a new name became urgent. There was one obvious choice, which had already been used by Ford, and which emphasised the car's sporting/lifestyle appeal. That name was Capri, left on the shelf after the 1964 departure of the two-door Consul Capri. In November 1967, the Capri name was officially adopted.

Back in the engineering departments, work was progressing fast. There were considerable concerns over the suspension. Because of the necessity for a low-slung, sleek shape, suspension travel had to be as short as possible to make the car sit down low. Reconciling the conflicting needs of sharp handling and an acceptable ride proved to be no easy task for the development team.

The classic Ford suspension package was used: MacPherson suspension was specified up front, while at the rear there was the familiar leaf-sprung live axle.

During Arctic shake-down testing in Finland in 1968 the rear window shape is still squared-off (right), while in hot-house conditions in Tunisia later that year the production-style C-shaped rear pillar has been approved (below).

This curious shot from deep within the Ford archives shows heavily disguised pre-production Capris being air-freighted by British Air Ferries in 1968.

However, the axle differed from the installation on other Fords in being located by radius arms. Telescopic dampers were the best medium for preventing the leaf springs from twisting, eliminating axle tramp. In Britain, engines were pulled from existing sources: the 1298cc unit came from the freshly launched Escort, the 1599cc engine was shared with the Cortina and the 1996cc V4 engine came from the Corsair. Gearboxes also came from the Cortina.

In the days before globalisation and the much-vaunted 'World Car' syndrome, Capris developed in Cologne were to have a number of unique features. In particular, the German engine range was different, having been developed independently in Germany to suit the Taunus models. The entire launch range of Cologne engines was therefore in V-form – V4s of 1305cc, 1498cc and 1698cc, and V6s of 1998cc and 2293cc. Gearboxes and final drives

were also mostly different from British Capris, but otherwise there were very few distinguishing features.

Everything was set for launch on 5 February 1969. In the event Ford's development budget had grown to £22 million, and the Capri had become a sizeable gamble. The big question was this: would European customers bite the ponycar bullet in the same way as Americans had done five years before?

CAPRI MK1 IN DETAIL

The first time the Capri was seen publicly was on 21 January 1969 at a special ceremony in the politically significant capital of Germany, Bonn, not too far from the Cologne plant. This preview went ahead despite the fact that the car was not scheduled to go on sale until 5 February.

Another chance for a sneak preview of the car the motoring press was falling over itself to cover came on the very last day of the Brussels Show, on 24 January 1969. A giant silver box wrapped in a ribbon tauntingly hid the actual car (although in fact you could see under it because the box was bottomless). Five TV screens around the stand flashed ½sec images of the new car – just enough to see the basic outline. Notices proclaimed that this was 'the car of your wildest dreams'.

Like many magazines, *Autocar* had been invited to a special pre-launch test event in Cyprus. When it learned that the embargo for releasing details on the new car was timed to coincide with the Brussels preview on 24 January, a Friday, it took the extraordinary step of delaying publication by one day from its usual Thursday so that it could give full coverage to the new Ford. The issue immediately sold out.

At the press preview of the Capri in Cyprus, Ford made available this Cosworth BDA-engined car for test. Note its wide Minilite wheels, round foglamps and bonnet bulge (the first example of a bulgy Capri). The writers liked it but it was destined to remain in prototype form, since the forthcoming V6 looked a better production bet.

In its launch statement, Ford actually tried to persuade everyone that Capri was pronounced as in the Italian, with the emphasis on the first syllable. English press hacks were used to the more familiar Anglo-Saxon holidaymaker pronunciation, which naturally prevailed in Britain.

Production had actually begun, somewhat later than hoped, in November 1968. The plan was that a healthy number of cars would be available for the launch date of 5 February 1969. By that stage, the Halewood plant in Liverpool was churning out 350 cars per day, with Cologne producing a similar number for continental markets. Despite some problems – strikes among component suppliers during December 1968 sent production at Halewood tumbling to just four cars per hour – such stocking up meant that there were enough

The all-new Capri was launched in February 1969, with a huge range of trim options. This is a top-spec GT XLR (above) – all those letters denoted that all option packs had been ordered. Portugal was the location for pre-launch photo shoots.

Lifestyle was heavily promoted (below), following the lead of the Mustang's 'personal coupe'.

Typical Ford strengths of comfortable seating, through-flow ventilation and clear fascia layout made the Capri an inviting place to be, although the fake wood effect was perhaps not so welcome. Base models had only two dials.

GT models gained a more comprehensive dash, including an extra four minor gauges and a centre console, plus extra rocker switches for the fog lamps if you had the R pack. Seating was also superior.

Capris for one to be delivered to every Ford dealership on launch day. But supplies for customers were a little thin on the ground – not entirely surprising when demand exceeded forecasted sales by a ratio of two-to-one. All this conspired to delay the launch of the more up-market 2.0-litre V4 and 3.0-litre V6 versions.

The press were treated to that pre-launch trip to Cyprus to try the full range of launch Capris. In fact, there were more than the full launch complement, since the test fleet included 2.0-litre V4 cars (which took several months to reach the market) and a batch of eight specially converted 1600GTs with Cosworth BDA 1600cc 16-valve engines. These unique 'Cossie' Capris had glass-fibre bonnets with bulges, Minilite 6in wheels and special exhausts, and their engines developed 122bhp at 6000rpm. The 16-valve Capri, however, would never reach the public: the engine was too harsh and complex, and a BDA Capri would not have made sense alongside the 3.0-litre V6.

For 1969, the big range of engine options was unprecedented for the European market. In Britain, all engines derived from models currently in production. Unlike the German range, these featured the usual British Ford design of Heron head pistons. At the bottom of the pile was the 1300 unit, a straight transfer from the Escort. It developed a lowly 52bhp in standard tune and a surprisingly effective 64bhp in GT specification, with a higher compression ratio and Weber carburation. Then came the 1600 units, taken directly from the Cortina. Again there were two states of tune: standard 64bhp and, in GT form with 9.2:1 compression ratio and a twin-

The 1300L was a lowly model in the range, and the 1300 engine was never really up to the job of moving a one-ton 'sporting' coupé around. The L pack added side louvres, wheel trims, bright side strip, bumper overriders and identifying L badges.

choke Weber carburettor, 82bhp. Listed at launch but not actually produced until March 1969, the 2000 engine was the V4 unit used in the Corsair, although for its role in the Capri it received enlarged inlet manifolds and porting. Ford quoted 110bhp, although this figure was SAE, not DIN like the others; the appropriate figure was actually 92.5bhp.

Gearboxes for British Capris derived from the Cortina, with its rather spaced-out set of ratios. For the 1600GT and 2000GT models, the Corsair 2000E/Cortina GT gearbox internals were fitted, with far more suitable close-set ratios. Each model had its own final drive, ranging from a lowly 4.125:1 for the base 1300s to a tallish 3.545:1 for the 2000GT.

On the suspension side, the independent front end followed text-book Ford practice with rubber-located MacPherson struts, dampers, track control arms and an anti-roll bar across the bottom. The rear end had caused all sorts of problems in development because of the insistence on a 'back end down' stance and the general lack of space for suspension travel. To keep costs down, semi-elliptic leaf springs – each with four leaves – had been specified on each side to suspend the live axle. To prevent twisting through torque and braking forces, a

Space in the rear was pretty limited in terms of both head and leg room. Base model (above left) had a single bench rear seat. Plusher models (above) had separate bucket rear seats. Despite the C-shaped rear window, the rear pillars were still very thick, leaving the rear area unpopular with claustrophobics.

Boot space and access was not a strong suit on Mk1 Capris, as this 1600XL demonstrates: the modest 8.2cu ft boot had a high lip and a narrow opening.

Another advantage of the Capri's long nose was the large crumple zone it provided in a crash. The thick rear pillars also made the car exceptionally rigid for its day.

This cutaway drawing of a 1600GT displays the MacPherson strut front suspension and leaf-sprung rear with its twin dampers which prevented the axle twisting under torque.

system of twin dampers was used, one fore and one aft of the axle, which was located by radius arms.

The steering was a positive rack and pinion system. The steering column was made collapsible to comply with US safety standards, and there were flexible joints in the column. As for the brakes, the Capri benefited from discs up front, while self-adjusting drums were standard at the rear across the range, albeit in two different diameters: the 1300 had 8in × 1.5in Cortina drums, while the others received 9in × 1.75in Corsair units. When the 2000GT and 3000GT arrived, they had slightly larger front discs too (9.625in versus 9.59in). A servo came only on the 1600GT and 2000GT, although for lesser models it was listed as an option.

The normal fuel tank, located over the rear axle, had a capacity of 10½ gallons (48 litres). In Germany all but the very base versions used a larger tank of 12¾ gallons (58 litres). It took until the launch of the 3.0-litre Capri in Britain for a larger tank of 13½ gallons (61 litres) to arrive in the UK, and then only for the 3000.

Overall dimensions mirrored other Ford models. The wheelbase was the same as the Corsair but length was virtually the same as the Cortina, so the Capri had comparatively short front and rear overhangs, which certainly helped appearances. The long nose made the Capri a safe car in a crash, while Ford also vaunted the strength provided by the rear pillars and the padded steering wheel as safety features.

In terms of space, the interior was roughly the same size as an Escort, although the lack of rear seat leg and head room was a definite shortcoming, and the front seats had limited travel for tall drivers. Ford suggested that five people could be seated in a Capri, but perhaps passengers expected less space than they do today; the interior was hardly sufficient for four, let alone five. Boot space, too, was rather limited at 8.2cu ft (0.23cu m), and the boot opening was small.

All Capris benefited from through-flow ventilation,

There was certainly no shortage of space in the Capri's engine bay: this engine looks positively lost. It is a 1600GT unit with twin Webers and an output of 82bhp – one of the most popular engine choices.

comfortable seating and a typically clear fascia layout. The penchant for fake wood veneer was present in the recessed instrument panel and, in higher specification models, the centre console.

At launch, it was claimed, correctly, that more options were on offer than for any other British car ever. The idea was based on the 'design-it-yourself' concept of the Mustang, which had proved so successful in America. The more options you have, the more a customer feels he has the right car for him. Such a mix-and-match policy led to there being no fewer than 26 quoted models available at launch in Britain (see page 75 for the full listing).

To look at it cynically, one could say that this was pure hype to increase profits, and that very few people in fact ever bought a basic Capri. With a few options taken into account, the keen pricing of the Capri range did not look such a bargain. Perhaps Ford heeded such comments because the option pack approach was dropped after about 18 months and many of the extras in the option packs were incorporated as standard equipment.

There were initially three basic option groups: X, L and R. The X pack predominantly comprised interior features and retailed at £32 12s 10d. It consisted of reclining front seats, a shaped rear bench seat, dipping rear view mirror, handbrake-on warning light, extra interior lamp, twin horns and a pair of reversing lamps. The L pack (£15 0s 4d) consisted of identifying badges, bumper overriders, bright wheel trims, bright metal dummy air scoops, locking filler cap and bright metal side mouldings. The R pack (£39 3s 4d) was only offered on GT models and consisted of 5in Rostyle wheels, 15in diameter leather-trimmed sports steering wheel with a large centre

boss, fog and spot lamps and a map reading light on a flexible stalk; your car also received matt black treatment for the bonnet, sills and tail panel unless you told Ford you did not want this.

In theory packs could be bought individually, but in practice the X pack nearly always came as a build-up to the L pack to make an XL, which was sold at a discounted combined price to encourage take-up. Consequently there was no such thing as an XR or LR. The almost mythical combination of all three packs made an XLR – again sold as a 'bulk buy' package at a discounted price of £79 12s 10d.

GT buyers could also expect some extra standard equipment: a three-spoke steering wheel, contoured seating, six gauges (instead of the usual two), two-speed wipers and extra rocker switches for the spot/fog lamps if you went for the R pack. Optional extras included a Ford-approved Golde folding sunroof (distributed in the UK by Allard) and inertia reel seat belts. A radio was a £31 option, its position being above the heater sliders, properly built into the fascia. Automatic transmission, always a Borg Warner 35 three-speeder for Mk1 Capris, was listed as an £89 option from the start, but only for the 1600, 2000 and 3000 models in the UK.

In line with Ford's stated aim of high value for the Capri, prices at launch began at just £890 for the base 1300. Even the up-market Capris were remarkably cheap: the 1600GT was £1042, the 2000GT was £1088 and a fully-loaded 2000GT XLR could be yours for £1167. To give some comparison, in February 1969 a Fiat 124 Coupé cost £1438, a Sunbeam Rapier £1337, an MGB GT £1217 and a Reliant Scimitar GTE £1797. None of these cars was really a direct competitor for the Capri, which began to carve its own market niche.

The celebrated international advertising campaign

The British 2000GT model, first available a few months after the 1300 and the 1600, used the Corsair's V4 engine. It developed 92.5bhp and was for a short while the most powerful engine in the Capri range.

The immortal advertising line for the Capri at launch: 'The car you always promised yourself'. Prices were kept deliberately at bargain level – just £890 for the base 1300, although few people actually spent so little, most opting for bigger engines and more gear.

Ford Capri: £890.

We don't want to mislead you. £890 buys you the Capri 1300.

The 1300 in the picture is fitted with optional sports road wheels, which naturally adds to the cost of the car.

But that doesn't really matter too much. The important thing about the car is this: whichever engine you decide on, 1300, 1300GT, 1600, 1600GT or 2000GT (just for the record, a 2000GT XLR is the most expensive Capri, it costs £1167), your Capri will have 4 things in common with every other Capri.

That beautiful shape.

Enough room in the back for 2 or 3 people to make themselves comfortable.

A good sized boot.

And a very sporty feel to it.

The rest is largely up to you. Because for the Capri we've worked out a system which gives you much more say in what you have in and on your car.

Depending on the version you choose, there's a Capri Custom Plan, that's a pack of extra equipment, which enables you to tailor your car pretty much to your own particular requirements.

Unfortunately, we can't say much about the best part of the bargain. How it feels when you first get behind the wheel of a Capri.

So instead we're going to suggest that you trip down to your nearest Ford dealer and arrange for a test drive.

All it needs is a quick trip round the houses. You'll come back sold.

Ford Capri: the car you always promised yourself.

CAPRI

boldly stated the Capri was 'the car you always promised yourself', adding: 'The new Ford Capri is the kind of car you've probably been hoping someone would make ever since you first put foot to clutch pedal'. Adverts were emblazoned in colour in magazines and in prominent poster positions in a concerted three-week long campaign which cost £125,000 in the UK alone.

In terms of sales, the Capri immediately grabbed a 3 per cent share of the entire car market in Britain, and

around 3.5 per cent in Germany – double the original forecast. The first production landmark was reached in just over one year on sale when the 250,000 mark was passed. While such runaway sales would soon drop off in Germany, Britain proved to be a more robust market, a situation that would continue right into the 1980s. One significant explanation for the early decline of the Capri in Germany was the launch of the very competent Opel Manta as a direct rival to the Capri.

The V6 arrives.................................

The Mustang-inspired long bonnet that gave the Capri such presence also provided plenty of room in the engine bay. There was obviously space for a fairly meaty motor to go in, and Ford had a natural in the 3.0-litre 'Essex' V6 engine developed for the Zodiac saloon. Plans for the V6 installation were laid surprisingly late in the day, the management go-ahead not having been given until late 1968.

For installation in the Capri, the V6 engine was strengthened slightly. To cope with the extra weight and power, a stronger cross-member with three mounting points, rather than two, held the engine in place. The front side members were reinforced and extra plates were welded into the top strut mountings. To clear the higher engine, a bonnet bulge was included, similar to that seen on the pre-production Cosworth BDA models.

The springs were stiffened front and rear, the dampers made firmer and the anti-roll bar bushes harder. Wider 185/70 tyres were specified, and the fuel tank capacity rose to 13½ gallons (61 litres) – although at the expense of luggage space, which dropped from 8.2cu ft (0.23cu m) to an even more meagre 7.8cu ft (0.22cu m). Other changes included twin exhaust tail-pipes, a larger radiator, an uprated battery and revised brake pads and linings.

The 3000GT was launched in October 1969 at a cost of £1291. The V6 engine's considerable power, an optimistic 144bhp SAE at 4740rpm (in other words about 136bhp DIN, later revised to 128bhp), was welcome, and its wide-based torque curve – with a maximum of 165lb ft at 3000rpm – even more so. Performance was very impressive: a claimed top speed of 114mph and 0-60mph in 9.2secs, or, with automatic transmission, 110mph and 0-60 in 11.4secs. The car also benefited from larger (2.25in wide) rear drums.

However, there was plenty of criticism about the gearbox. Although the casting was new, the internals were essentially from the Zodiac and that meant they were designed to lug 23½cwt of metal around. Raising the final drive to 3.22:1 for the Capri scarcely helped because of the cavernous gaps between ratios. The two-piece propshaft and the rear axle were inherited from German Capris, and a larger clutch was standard. The familiar three-speed Borg Warner 35 automatic gearbox was a popular option.

The 3000GT was joined in March 1970 by the even more up-market 3000E. The E stood for Executive, Ford's moniker for swank at the time, denoting its luxury bias. As well as most of the usual XLR extras, the E added a vinyl roof, push-button radio, heated rear window, opening rear quarter windows and cloth inserts for the seats. It cost £1513, a £91 premium over the 3000GT XLR.

The tuner's art.................................

Some owners were already impatient to get more from their Capri, and a whole industry sprang up to satisfy such needs. Before the arrival of Ford's own 3000, a company called Piranha offered a 3.0-litre V6 conversion with a different gearbox which gave quicker acceleration times.

Legendary tuners Broadspeed made a conversion for the 1600GT, consisting of a twin-choke carburettor (which boosted power by 20bhp), lowered suspension, 6in Minilite wheels and a front spoiler, all painted in Broadspeed's obligatory Regal Red and Georgian Silver paint scheme. You could expect 0-60mph in about the same time as a 3000GT and a top speed approaching 110mph. It was expensive, but a spectacular performer and a sharp handler. Broadspeed also went on to modify 3.0-litre Capris to great effect, starting with the 175bhp Bullit and culminating in a monster turbocharged road car that echoed some Ford AVO experiments.

SuperSpeed went a different route by fitting a Mustang Boss 302 V8 engine into the Capri's cavernous engine bay. One example even used a 5.7-litre Boss V8 with a gulping 380bhp on tap – surely the ultimate road Capri. Alan Allard did the same sort of thing with a 225bhp 302 V8 engine for around £1700. Like many V8 conversions, handling suffered because a V8 engine was so much heavier than was ever intended in a Capri. Allard also made a name for himself bolting superchargers on to V6 engines, giving 180-190bhp for about £250.

Jeff Uren of RaceProved marketed Weslake's tuning kits for the 3000GT, basically spin-offs of Ford's early experiments in racing. Various kits were offered, including the 170 (indicating the brake horsepower available) with its modified camshaft, porting and carburettor jets, and the 190 (also known as the Commanche) with its big valves, high compression ratio, new camshaft and new exhaust – and an ability to do 0-60mph sprints in 6.6secs. Uren also went the V8 route, producing the legendary Stampede. This was fitted with a standard 285bhp American Ford V8, which gave 0-60mph in 5.8secs!

Yet another name which became famous for converting Capris was Lumo. They got an easy 170-180bhp from the 3.0-litre engine and upgraded other areas such as Spax adjustable rear dampers and uprated twin exhausts.

Tuners were soon pouncing on the Capri to satisfy a burgeoning go-faster market. This is an effort on a 3000GT from Lumo, which offered around 180bhp for modest outlay. The wide arches and bonnet mascot are a touch of frippery.

E.D. Abbott's convertible conversion was an attractive route to open-topped motoring, if costly at prices from £1442. Crayford made a similar car and even Ford considered making a production drop-top Capri.

It was not just the performance tuning brigade which pounced on the Capri. The first company to make a convertible Capri was coachbuilder E.D. Abbott, which made a handful of cars to its own design. This mirrored a conversion by Carbodies that Ford had sponsored; at one stage there was talk of producing a Ford-catalogued convertible. At Earls Court in October 1971 celebrated conversion specialists Crayford Cars also displayed an elegant drop-top Capri, which they would call the Caprice. Crayford converted a total of 30 such cars to a very high standard. Crayford's experience with the Capri had also included, in 1969, a short run of high-powered

cars for the Spanish market: the Eliminator (which pre-empted Ford's fitment of the Zodiac V6 engine) and the Exterminator (with 5-litre Ford Windsor V8 power). Only 31 of these ferociously-named creatures were built.

Another company called Thoroughbred Sports Cars also made a decent trade in converting Capris to pick-ups! This began in the early days but reached its zenith in 1981 when it offered a conversion called the Bobcat, designed by Richard Oakes and featuring new glass-fibre body panels and an optional 5.3-litre V8.

The Mk1's production changes·········

Back with Ford, the whole Capri range was overhauled in September 1970. The number of trim options was reduced drastically because Ford ceased to offer X, L and R option packs individually. Now only grouped-together packs – L, XL or (for GT models only) XLR – could be bought. The 1300 and 1600 engines received better carburation, reshaped cylinder head porting and new camshaft profiles, so their outputs all increased. The base 1300 unit went up by 5bhp to 57bhp, and the 1300GT stepped up by 8bhp to 72bhp; meanwhile the outputs of the 1600 and 1600GT engines rose by 4bhp to 68bhp and 86bhp respectively. Performance was subtly enhanced.

Also in September 1970, a brake servo was standardised across the range (except on the 1300). Other minor tweaks were new optional Lucas auxiliary lights and optional nylon upholstery.

The very first special edition Capri arrived in September 1971, rather unimaginatively called the Capri

The seminal 3000GT arrived in October 1969, immediately identifiable by its muscular bonnet bulge. Note the XLR specification of matt black bonnet and sills. This export model has extra indicators on the front wings. The torquey 'Essex' V6 engine developed around 128bhp and was good enough in the Capri for 114mph and 0-60mph in 9.2secs.

The all-important badges communicated all you needed to know to onlookers.

A new top-of-the-range model arrived in 1970: the 3000E (for Executive). This luxury version had most of the XLR equipment plus a vinyl roof, radio, opening rear quarter windows and cloth seats.

Special and based on the 2000GT XLR. What made it 'Special' were the inclusion of such period junk extras as rear window slats, matt black boot spoiler and vinyl roof, while more welcome was the cloth trim, heated rear window and radio. This proto-collectable could be had in any colour you liked as long as it was Vista Orange. Only 1200 Specials were produced.

In October 1971, at the Earls Court Motor Show, Ford announced revised engines for the 3000GT and 3000E. A new camshaft profile for the venerable V6 gave it the ability to rev more freely, while higher valve lift helped push up power, together with bigger inlet ports

and valves, reshaped inlet manifolding, enhanced-flow carburettor jets, viscous coupling for the cooling fan and a new exhaust.

Power was up to 138bhp DIN, a rise, said Ford, of 8 per cent. Torque rose only fractionally from an already impressive 173lb ft to 174lb ft at 3000rpm. Not only that, but emissions were claimed to have been significantly reduced. Other changes included softer rear springs, a bigger brake servo, larger auxiliary lights and a new design of spoked steel wheel. Also new was a higher final drive of 3.09:1 and a revised second gear ratio, bridging the previous abyss between second and third and at last imbuing the 3000 models with the sports car gearing they had craved. Performance was much improved. Ford claimed that the new 3000 models were 'the fastest production line cars ever to be sold by Ford in Britain'.

The very first Capri special edition was painted in obligatory orange and featured such oddities as rear window slats, special wheel trims and a matt black boot spoiler. Just 1200 Capri Specials were made.

In September 1972, the so-called Capri 'Mk1½' was launched. Exterior changes visible on the 1600XL (upper) included larger headlamps, indicators moved under the bumper and a new grille. As can be seen on the 1600GT (lower), the rear lamps were also enlarged and the dummy side louvres were made smaller. Under the skin, the 1600 used the Cortina overhead camshaft engine and all models gained better suspension.

Many of these changes, particularly regarding mechanicals and interiors, would persist into the Capri II of 1974-78 and even beyond.

The old 1600 overhead valve engine was dropped in favour of the Cortina MkIII 1600 overhead camshaft derivation of the familiar Pinto design. Again there was a standard version (producing 72bhp) and a twin-choke GT derivative (with 88bhp). An entry-level 1300 model was kept going, using the same engine (in Britain at least), but the 1300GT died at this point, since the standard 1600 performed just as well with less fuss. The 2000GT V4 engine was kept going with no changes, a decision having been made not to use the 2.0-litre Pinto in-line four from the Cortina because of supply shortages. For the 3.0-litre Capri, the lanky old Zodiac 'box was replaced with the much more suitable German Consul/Granada unit, which also tended to baulk less severely.

Mechanically, all models received much softer spring rates (especially the V6) and increased suspension travel, and shed their rear suspension radius rods in favour of a new cranked rear anti-roll bar. Since this anti-roll bar was so narrow (only 10mm diameter) and only about half the length of the axle, its efficacy was never very great. A tendency of late-model Mk1 Capris, therefore, was to wallow at the back end. Additionally, all models were now fitted with 5in wide wheels as standard.

Exterior changes included new and much bigger sealed-beam headlamps with the indicators moved from

Quoted top speed was up 8mph to 122mph and the 0-60mph time tumbled to just 8.3secs.

The 3000GT lasted only a few more months, with the last one made in February 1972; the 3000E ceased production in July 1972, in readiness for its replacement in September by a new model called the 3000GXL, which formed part of a completely overhauled range.

So far the only British production Capris to have that beacon of 1970s automotive libido, a bonnet bulge, were the 3.0-litre models. In June 1972, Ford launched a hat-trick of Capri Specials which presaged the spread of bonnet-bulginess to lesser Capris. Based on the 1600GT, 2000GT or 3000GT, these Specials not only had the requisite bulge, but a heated rear window, cloth trim, opening rear quarter windows, hazard flashers, inertia reel seat belts, matt black dash and a centre console. The choice of colours this time was Ebony Black or Emerald Green, with contrasting coachlines in red or gold.

In September 1972, the whole Capri range was given a thorough shake-up. Capris made in this period are sometimes referred to as the 'Mk1½' because the changes were so far-reaching. Ford claimed that there were no fewer than 151 improvements in the overhauled Capri.

the headlamps to a new position under the front bumper, new and bigger tail light clusters with built-in reversing lights, smaller dummy side louvres, new front grilles and a power bulge for all models. Every Capri except the base 1300 was now fitted with radial ply tyres.

An all-new Granada-inspired dash graced the interior, incorporating a drop-down glovebox for the first time and a more convincing wood veneer effect. Other changes were a new two-spoke steering wheel, new style switchgear and larger white-on-grey instruments. A centre console became standard on GT and GXL models. The seats were reshaped to give more of a bucket effect and ½in of extra legroom was freed for rear passengers by hollowing out the backs of the front seats. All models now had cloth seat inserts instead of being all-plastic as before.

New trim level names were introduced (L, XL, GT and GXL) and the range was considerably pared back. There were now only one 1300 (L), three 1600s (L, XL and GT), a single 2000GT and a new 3000GXL flagship. There remained a Rally decor group for GT models, consisting of sports wheels, twin auxiliary lamps, side stripe, map reading light and leather gear knob.

The new range-topping 3000GXL was advertised as the 'Leader of the Pack' with a horse and hounds scenario in the background – surely Gary Glitter had more relevance in the Capri's case? The GXL was certainly plush: it had many of the Rally decor group items, such as sports road wheels, but added its own distinctive features of American-style quad headlamps, a chrome strip following the hockey-stick accent and opening rear quarter windows. By now the 3.0-litre engine's output was quoted at 140bhp.

Yet this was not the ultimate British Mk1 Capri. That honour went to the RS3100 (described on page 32), which did not enter production until the end of 1973 and was still very much current when the Capri II was launched in February 1974. Capri Mk1 production ceased at Halewood with a final batch of 384 cars in January 1974. By this stage, production of the Capri II was already in full swing.

Capri in Germany ....

The 1968 Escort and earlier Transit van had blazed the trail for co-operation between Ford of Britain and Ford of Germany, being essentially common products in both countries. The Capri was the next logical step, to be produced not only in Britain at Halewood but also in Germany at Ford's sizeable plant in Cologne – and before long at Saarlouis as well.

Simultaneously developed with its UK-built equivalent, the Cologne-built Capri was essentially the same beast at a cursory glance. Cosmetically there was very little to tell between the ranges, but under the skin there were some important differences. Chief among these were the power plants: Ford of Germany naturally chose to fit the engines it was then building for its Taunus range of saloons.

At launch in February 1969, Cologne-built Capris came with a choice of three four-cylinder engines: 1300, 1500 and 1700. All were unique to German production, and all were V4 configuration with flat-top pistons, an engine type that dated back to 1962. The base 1305cc unit developed 50bhp, the 1498cc 60bhp (65bhp from September 1970) and the 1699cc 75bhp.

German Fords were the first production Capris to be fitted with a V6 option. The first V6 arrived in May 1969 in the form of a 2.0-litre unit (with either 85bhp or 90bhp) and a bigger-bore 2.3-litre V6 (108bhp). They were of a totally different family from the 'Essex' V6 engines, having flat-top pistons and vertical valves in conventional combustion chambers. All German units, whether V4 or V6, shared common ancestry, the V6 units simply having an extra pair of cylinders added to one end.

German Capris were characterised by sweeter running engines on the whole, thanks to the vee format. They also had slightly smaller front disc brake sizes and marginally stiffer springs and dampers. Externally the differences were minor. One distinguishing feature was that the use of a bonnet bulge was more common on German Capris than British ones – the plain 2000, for example, had one from the word go.

Launch prices ranged from DM6993 for the no-frills 1300 up to DM8965 for the 2300GT; such prices were very cheap compared with other cars of sporting pretension. As in Britain, the same X and L option packs were on offer. The R pack was only available on Capri GT models (1700 and 2300) or on a special version of the 2000; this included a higher compression engine developing an extra 5bhp (the more powerful 90bhp engine became standard from 1970). German R models also had more extensive matt black treatment than the British equivalents, featuring this finish for windscreen pillars and window surrounds.

By the end of 1969, the Capri had sold 76,443 examples in Germany. The most popular model initially was the 1700 (31,712 sales in 1969), followed by the 1500 (23,109) and the 1300 (10,052). Automatic transmission was available from the Frankfurt Motor Show of September 1969 on all models from the 1500 up to the

Revised 'Mk1½' interior included a new dashboard with larger instruments, drop-down glovebox and two-spoke steering wheel. The seats were reshaped with a deeper bucket, and now had cloth inserts instead of being all-plastic.

2300GT. Also the first and reverse ratios of the four-speed manual gearbox were slightly altered at the same time; final drive ratios also differed from British Capris.

More news in September 1969 was the launch of an additional 2300GT model alongside the original 108bhp version. This gained an extra 17bhp to take the engine's output up to 125bhp. Claimed performance for this exciting newcomer was 185kph (115mph) top speed and 0-100kph (0-62mph) in around 10secs. This 125bhp version lasted only until August 1970 because, the following month, it was replaced by a new 2600GT model which delivered 125bhp more reliably and with stronger torque. The 2.6-litre engine was simply a stroked version of the 2.3-litre V6, and was already in production for the Taunus 26M.

More changes to the range occurred in September 1970. The scheme of L, X and R option packs was rationalised in line with the UK, so that options now encompassed L, XL and XLR. The lesser (85bhp) version of the 1998cc engine was dropped and the 1498cc engine received a higher compression ratio to boost power by 5bhp, to 65bhp. By this stage, 250,000 Capris had been made in Cologne, double the output of Halewood. And that proportion would continue: with a Capri line coming into action at the Saarlouis factory in 1970, output was usefully increased still further. It was at the

Saarlouis plant that celebrations for the millionth Capri (an RS2600) occurred in late 1973.

Tuners were just as keen on the Capri in Germany as they were in Britain. Perhaps the most celebrated of the early tuners – because he obtained official approval from Ford of Germany and sold his conversion through selected Ford dealers – was Michael May. He was the first person to turbocharge a Capri, using an Eberspächer-Bosch turbo unit in conjunction with the 2.3-litre V6 engine. The upshot was an engine with 180bhp on tap – but that was with a rev limiter fitted. Without the limiter it was capable of developing up to 240bhp! The 180bhp turbo conversion was homologated with uprated suspension and brakes and retailed for the equivalent of £325. Later a snorting 250bhp version was marketed for a cost of about 60 per cent more, and competition-minded customers lapped them up.

For 1972, Ford launched a pair of limited edition Capris in Germany. One was based on the 1500 and was painted Monza Blue, the other on the 1700GT in Corn

A plush new top model arrived in September 1972: the 3000GXL boasted American-style quad headlamps, a chrome side strip and opening rear quarter lights. This was the most expensive Capri yet at £1831. First German promotional leaflet for the Capri was simple and to the point. The motto inside was similar to the British ad line, reading: 'A car that you have always wished for'.

Yellow. Standard features included sports wheels with 165-13 tyres, matt black sills, rear panel and grille, two-tone horn, heated rear window and vinyl roof; 1000 examples of each were made.

The biggest change in the German Mk1 Capri's life occurred in September 1972. Finally the exclusively vee-format line-up of engines came to end in Germany. The old 1305cc V4 was replaced by a new overhead camshaft 1293cc in-line four from the Taunus (developing 55bhp), an engine offered only in markets supplied by Germany – and then only for one season.

The old vee-form 1500, 1700 and 2000 engines were phased out in favour of just one new engine – the overhead 1599cc in-line four launched simultaneously in Britain. There were two states of tune, as in the UK: 72bhp and (with GT badges) 88bhp. Lastly the 3.0-litre engine finally became available in the German market, rated at 140PS at 5300rpm. Thus the range was pared down to just seven models: 1300L, 1600XL, 1600GT, 2300GT, 2600GT, RS2600 and 3000GXL.

Der neue Capri.

An absolutely plain base Capri was a rare sight, but here is one (upper): no wheel trims, no louvres, no fancy badging. The 1300cc V4 engine fitted to this Cologne-built Capri came from the Taunus and was quite different from Halewood-built cars, as indeed was the entire range of engines. The 1972 1700GT (lower) used a 1699cc V4 engine developing 75bhp and could reach a top speed of 95mph. Note the slightly more generous use of matt black on this German car than on British Capris: it overlaps the bonnet and surrounds the glasshouse.

Production of the Mk1 Capri ended in Germany in December 1973, although records appear to show, somewhat strangely, that the last Mk1 car was produced on 31 October 1974, and one final RS2600 was recorded as having been produced in 1975. The final tally of Mk1 output at the Cologne Niehl and Saarlouis plants reached 784,000 Mk1s. Only a third of that production was sold on the German market (244,000 units); the remainder was exported, mostly to America.

RS Capris

In Ford-speak, RS means Rallye Sport. That magical combination of letters first appeared in January 1970 on the legendary Escort RS1600, the first production car to receive the Cosworth BDA engine which, as described above (see page 15), had been fitted to a pre-production batch of Capris. The RS1600 was initially built at Halewood, but production transferred later that year to Ford's Advanced Vehicle Operations (AVO) department. Based in South Ockenden, Essex, AVO was set up partly to ease the disruption at Halewood caused by making such a specialised car.

Although the first edition of Ford's RS Capri was produced exclusively in Germany, its birthplace was at AVO HQ in Essex. A small team headed by Ray Horrocks and Bob Howe did most of the development work to a brief set by Jochen Neerpasch, Ford's competitions chief in Germany. The need for an RS Capri was pressing, because Neerpasch wanted to homologate the Capri for racing in Germany. His brief called for a car which could be homologated to contemporary regulations: a weight of only 900kg (even the German base model 1300 weighed a not insubstantial 975kg) and an engine that could be adapted to international class standards (that meant around 2.6 litres).

The green light for the project was not received until November 1969 and the brief was to get a car ready for the Geneva Salon in March the following year – a task which was completed with predictable brinkmanship. The prototype RS2600 duly appeared at the show, but with a dummy engine! Despite the rush, by April 1970 Ford's Pilot Plant at Niehl had constructed 50 RS2600s in anticipation of competition homologation, which was achieved in October 1970.

To keep the weight down, prototypes were stripped of their heaters, carpets and bumpers. Meanwhile the doors, bonnet and boot lid were made from glass-fibre and the rear and side windows were in Perspex. Hence the first RS2600 quickly gained the nickname 'Plastikbombe'.

In Germany the top Capri was the 2600GT XLR, offered from 1970. With 125bhp on tap, it was nearly as fast as a 3.0-litre Capri – 118mph (190kph) and 0-60mph in under 10secs. The advert for the German 2300GT Automatic (above right) flaunts its quick shifting nature. In practice, the automatic Capri was slow to shift in the showroom.

Homologation cars for road use, however, would be much heavier and would have all-steel bodywork, although some of the weight-paring measures were retained. The wheels chosen were light magnesium 6in Richard Grant alloys, bumpers remained absent to start with, and even the paintwork was reduced to three layers...

The German 26M 2.6-litre engine was used as the basis for the RS2600. It gained a long-throw crank to expand its capacity to 2637cc, but, most importantly, it received the first ever fuel injection system fitted to a production Ford. This mechanical injection system was manufactured by Kügelfischer; the injection pump was mounted high up on the right-hand side of the engine and crank-driven by an internal cogged belt. However, the development work was done in Britain by Weslake.

The 2.6-litre engine also received a higher 10.0:1 compression ratio, a different exhaust with twin tail pipes, cast alloy inlet manifolds and prominent alloy plenum chamber, hot camshaft and beefed-up sump. The net result was an engine which, in standard road tune, developed 150bhp at 5800rpm and 166lb ft of torque at 3500rpm. And it was all delivered in a smooth and effortless way.

There were naturally changes to the suspension. The front crossmember was modified to move the suspension arms outwards for negative camber, while the front springs were stiffer. At the back, competition single leaf springs worked in conjunction with Bilstein gas dampers. Brakes were standard Capri, as was the four-speed gearbox (with a long-legged 3.22:1 final drive).

Aesthetically, the new RS2600 looked like it had true purpose. Its four US-style headlamps sat in a nose subtly reshaped to accommodate inset indicators, and the front arches were lightly flared. Initially there were no bumpers and no front spoiler, though both would be fitted later in the model's career. At the rear, twin separate-exit exhausts looked the part, and the bumperless treatment meant fitting stand-alone number plate lights. Tests demonstrated a Cd figure of 0.40.

The RS2600 really had no need for the tacky decor packages of lesser Capris, so it did without dummy

RS stood for Rallye Sport – and the RS2600 lived up to those initials. Light weight was the key theme for the first RS model: no bumpers, light alloy wheels and a lack of external adornment.

louvres, chrome strips, auxiliary lamps and fancy badging. The usual matt black treatment was present on most cars – on the bonnet (stretching round the front pillars and glasshouse), sills and rear panel. The simple RS badges were the epitome of restraint.

With their steel doors, bonnet and boot, the production cars weighed 1060kg, compared with the homologation 900kg for the racing 'Plastikbombe' cars with their glass-fibre opening panels. Ironically the RS2600 was the heaviest of all German Mk1 Capris, except the V6 automatics, so it was not the lightning fast machine it might have been. Still, the factory claim of 0-100kph (0-62mph) in 8.6secs and a top speed of 200kph (125mph) was strong stuff for 1970. A German magazine actually tested one to 125.8mph and 0-62mph in only 7.7secs.

Inside, a stripped-out feel combined with a general upgrade of equipment. Some RS2600s had fixed-back bucket seats but most had special reclining Scheel bucket seats trimmed in black cord. The steering wheel was deeply dished and the six-dial dashboard contained a

220kph speedo and a tacho red-lined at 5800rpm. There was initially no centre console.

Full production began at Niehl in September 1970, with the first deliveries occurring one month later. The cars could be bought only at Ford Rallye Sport dealers and the cost was DM15,800, at a time when the 2300GT cost DM9980 – at some 50 per cent more, the RS2600 was a specialised machine. It sold across continental Europe but never made it to Britain, but then the UK did have the Capri 3000. A handful did in fact make it over the English Channel for the right Ford executives – and somehow a few even acquired right-hand drive!

Improvements to the RS2600 arrived in October 1971 with the introduction of a new AVO-styled four-spoke alloy wheel, which would eventually allow larger (9.75in) ventilated front discs and Granada calipers to be fitted. Also from the newly-launched Granada came the gearbox, which would also be fitted to the Capri 3000 from late 1972. Suspension was softened and the ride height raised. At the same time, chrome quarter bumpers were fitted at the front and a full bumper at the rear.

Other changes in the RS2600 life-cycle included matt black bumpers, auxiliary lamps, some rather tacky stripes for the bonnet and rear end, extra decals, new cloth upholstered front and rear seats, flat steering wheel and centre console. Like all Capris, it gained a rear anti-roll

The heart of the Cologne-built RS2600 was a stroked version of Ford's 2.6-litre V6, tweaked by Weslake and fitted with Kügelfischer fuel injection. Power output was 150bhp – the highest of any Mk1 Capri. The original interior of the RS2600 was very sparse: no centre console and optional radio for example. But you did get very attractive bucket seats and a deeply dished three-spoke steering wheel.

bar from autumn 1972. Towards the end of production, the gear ratios were restacked and the 3.09:1 final drive of the 3000 was introduced.

As a racing machine, the RS2600 was a fearsome beast, its engine being progressively bored out to 3.0 litres and its output growing year by year, from 265bhp in 1971 to 325bhp in 1973. The full achievements of the model are outlined in the chapter dealing with competition history (see pages 56–69). As a road car, too, the RS2600 was probably a greater success than Ford might have hoped. It was only offered to homologate Ford's racing programme, yet some 3532 cars had been built by the time the RS2600 ceased production in early 1974. By then, however, a new RS had come on line, this time produced in Britain – the RS3100.

Meanwhile Ferguson had built a number of four-wheel drive prototypes, including a batch of about a dozen cars for police evaluation. There had been serious consideration about producing the four-wheel drive rallycross Capri as a road car, but this was scotched at a late stage. Legend has it that, at a demonstration to Ford executives in the Alps, the prototype was parked nose-down on a snow-covered hill, and then failed to reverse up it, the four-wheel drive system unable to engage. The Ford execs left unimpressed...

The RS3100 was a different story. Here again, the requirement was for a homologation road car which the factory could develop into a race winner. The German 2.6-litre engine had been taken about as far as it could go by Weslake, so the 3.0-litre 'Essex' V6 was the natural choice for evolution. Cosworth Engineering was chosen for the job of developing and making the engines. Ford agreed with Cosworth that a bored-out 3.1-litre engine was a good basis for future racing: maintaining the standard 72.42mm stroke, it could be bored out to as much as 100mm (to make an engine of 3.4 litres).

The production RS3100 engine had a capacity of 3091cc and was claimed to develop 148bhp at 5200rpm. That was the result of Cosworth's porting developments, gas flowed head (with blue-coloured rocker covers) and a higher compression ratio. The fuel injection of the RS2600 was swapped for a single Weber 38 carburettor. In other words, the RS3100 engine was nothing very radical, and 148bhp was not that much higher than the standard Capri 3000GT (which was claimed to have 138bhp). Nevertheless, the RS3100 was notably quicker, with a top speed of 125mph and 0-60mph in a quoted 7.3secs (more like 7.8secs in reality).

Aerodynamics certainly played their part. Spoilers had never been homologated for the RS2600, but in light of BMW's success with aerodynamic aids on the 3.0CSL, AVO pressed ahead with adding a ducktail spoiler on the boot and a small lip spoiler at the front, which helped high-speed stability no end. Wind tunnel tests yielded a Cd figure of 0.37.

Underneath it all, though, the new RS3100 broke very little new ground. The suspension, brakes and 6in alloy wheels were carried over directly from the RS2600, with perhaps a slightly softer setting on the rear dampers. Nevertheless, the press attacked what was still an appalling ride; heavy steering and an unrefined engine note were the other main complaints. In other respects, the RS3100 was praised for its predictable handling and particularly its outstanding performance and impressive torque (187lb ft at 3000rpm).

Where the RS3100 differed most from the RS2600 was in its appearance. Many aspects were similar: it shared the RS2600's matt black bumpers (quarter bumpers at the front), quad headlamps, Ford AVO four-spoke wheels and front air dam. Its distinguishing features were the large matt black rear spoiler, the removal of 'injection' decals, dummy louvres, different badges and unique colour schemes (shared with AVO's Escort programme). The interior was pretty much stock 3000GXL, although a 130mph speedometer was fitted in the dash.

RS3100 production began in November 1973 at Halewood (and perhaps a few were made at Boreham). Production was intermittent at best, and actually overlapped with the Capri II. The RS3100 was homologated in January 1974 for the forthcoming season, and, despite the requirement for a minimum of 1000 examples, only 248 were officially completed.

It was an expensive road car at £2450 and unfortunately arrived at the worst possible time for such a performance machine. As the mid-1970s oil crisis dug in, this sort of car was utterly out of fashion in fuel-starved Britain. In any case, the RS3100 was almost obsolete as soon as it was launched, since the Capri II was imminent. Many RS3100s ended up being discounted to shift them and some hung around forecourts until the end of 1974.

The RS3100 served its purpose, however, enabling Ford to have a competitive car for the '74 season, even if it looked out-of-date alongside the new Capri II. RS3100s quickly gained the mantle of rare and prized collectors' cars as the fuel crisis waned and drivers looked at them for what they were.

Capri in America ....

The American chapter of the Capri story is often underplayed but its significance should never be underestimated. America was a huge market for the car and an avid following developed for it. The Capri was first shown in America at the New York Show in April 1970. Billed as the 'European Sporty Car' and as 'The Sexy European', it slotted neatly into Ford's North American marketing machine as a sub-species Mustang.

In stark contrast to the massive ranges offered in Europe, the very first Capris to come off the boat were of a single model: a 1600cc 'Kent'-engined version, offered in a single trim level. The 1600cc engine was a logical choice because it had already passed emissions tests. In US tune, it was slightly less powerful (71bhp gross).

The car was launched on 17 April 1970 simply as the Capri. It was distributed and serviced by dealers in the Lincoln-Mercury network, even though no Mercury badges actually appeared on the car: the lettering on the bonnet read simply 'Capri'. And the dealers did a good job: after the first month all supplies had been exhausted. The year ended with some 17,258 Capris having been sold, a level of success that reflected the car's image as almost more of a Mustang than the Mustang itself, which had already shed its smart origins to become something of a bloated monster. Ford was able to claim that the Capri had sold more examples in its first year in the US

The RS2600 was not imported to Britain but here is a UK registered example: some of Ford's top brass such as competitions manager Stuart Turner drove the quad-lamp Capri.

From 1971, the RS2600 got new AVO four-spoke alloys and chrome front quarter bumpers. Under the skin, the suspension became softer and a new Granada gearbox was fitted.

than any other import in history, and it was second only to the VW Beetle in the imported car sales charts.

Initially, engines, running gear and interiors were obtained from Halewood in Britain, and complete cars were shipped from Cologne. But a massive Ford strike in Britain in early 1971 really scotched Halewood as a reliable source of supply. Ford instead turned exclusively to Cologne for American exports, to the great benefit of production tallies in Germany.

Early Capris were sold in manual transmission form only – an odd decision given American buyers' natural preference for automatic. Options included a vinyl roof, air conditioning and a decor package. Federalisms included bumper overriders, grille-mounted amber

parking/signal lights and side repeaters. US Capris always had quad headlamps.

For 1971, a 2.0-litre engine was also offered, but instead of being one of the European units (V4 or V6) this was the Pinto overhead camshaft engine which would soon make it into the Cortina and Taunus. For American consumption it was rated at 100bhp (SAE), and automatic transmission became an option for the first time. Meanwhile, the manual-only 1600 got a 4bhp boost to 75bhp.

Road Test magazine voted the Capri 'Import Car of the Year' for 1971, while *Import Buyer's Guide* proclaimed: 'If any modern automotive product ever reaches the universality of the Model T, it will be the Capri'. Praise indeed.

For 1972, the 2.6-litre V6 engine arrived in America, albeit with 18bhp less than in Europe (at 107bhp). After 1972, the 1600 engine ducked out, leaving just the 2.0-litre four and 2.6-litre V6 engines. The '73 models (on sale from July 1972) had to suffer the aesthetic curse of Federal bumpers, which increased the overall length of the car by no less than 6in. At this stage they were still bright but had large overriders and rubber inserts.

The RS was a quick machine. One magazine tested the car to over 125mph and from rest to 62mph in just 7.7secs.

The final incarnation of the RS2600 had matt black bumpers and extra driving lamps. Over 3500 examples were built by the time production ended.

The bumpers gained a painted finish for the '74 model year, but the big change that year was the replacement of the 2.6-litre V6 with the 'Cologne' 2.8-litre V6, its first use in any Ford, predating installation in European Capris by some eight years (it was also fitted to the new Ford Mustang II at the same time). In US specification, this engine developed 105bhp (SAE), much less than Europeans could later expect.

The Capri Mk1 was a remarkable success in the US. From 1970 to the end of the 1975 model year, a total of 408,288 cars were sold there, the best year being 1973, when 113,069 were shifted. Indeed, the US and Canada together were the Capri's best market world-wide, taking about twice as many as the next best (Britain).

The British-built RS3100 resembled an RS2600 from the outside, although it had a big rear spoiler and items like dummy side louvres. It arrived very late in the Mk1's life just as the oil crisis bit, so it was doomed to a brief existence.

High flying in an RS3100 was easy enough, since it was capable of 0-60mph in around 7.5secs and could reach 125mph.

Unlike the RS2600, the RS3100 used an 'Essex' V6 engine, bored out and modified by Cosworth to produce 148bhp. The other major difference was the rejection of fuel injection in favour of a big Weber carburettor.

The large duck-tail rear spoiler can be seen well in this action shot.

Inside the RS3100 looked rather like a GXL but it boasted the latest flat-dish RS steering wheel and a speedo which read to 130mph.

Capri in South Africa.........................

Capris were also built in South Africa, and the undoubted star of the line-up was peculiar to that country. In 1970, Ford of South Africa officially did what many tuning firms tried in Britain: shoehorn a big V8 engine into the Capri. This was not an unusual practice in South Africa, where bags of American-style torque went down a treat.

The V8 Capri was created by a Johannesburg-based tuner and racer called Basil Green, who had already marketed a V6 Cortina MkII under the Perana name. Incidentally, Perana was a deliberate mis-spelling of the carnivorous fish. After careful evaluation by Ford Product Engineering in Johannesburg, the muscular Perana Capri V8 was deemed fit to bear Ford badges

European origins of the Capri were stressed when it arrived as a best-seller in America in 1970. Earliest versions (above) looked very much like German models, except for the quad headlamp nose, bumper overriders and extra lighting. Later US-specification Capris suffered from the Federal bumper treatment. By the time the '74 model year Capri came out (below), the 2.8-litre V6 engine had become available in the US only – its first use in a Capri, although it had a pitifully low power output compared with European engines.

In South Africa, Ford sold Capris with Mustang V8 engines under the name Perana. As well as making brutal road cars, they achieved phenomenal success on the track with the name Z181.

was an automatic option for the faint-hearted.

Other changes included lowered suspension, stiffer springs, quick-ratio steering rack (mounted to the bulkhead) and barely adequate Lotus Cortina disc brakes. Options included spoilers front and rear, louvres for the back window and even bonnet locking pins!

Between 1970 and 1973, when all Capri production ended in South Africa, just over 500 Peranas were built. That was enough to homologate the model for racing, and the Z181 wishbone-suspended competition Perana scored some notable successes, including taking the South African Championship three times in the hands of Basil Green. Indeed it was so fast in the 1970 season, taking 12 wins out of 13 starts, that it was, for a time, banned from racing altogether.

for the special needs of the South African market.

Green took an American Ford Mustang 302 (5.0-litre) V8 engine (actually fitted to locally-made Fairlanes) and found that it made a neat fit in the Capri's capacious engine bay. Adding only a solid lifter high-performance cam, special manifolds and a Holley four-barrel carburettor, the engine's output was a healthy 281bhp; torque of 300lb ft at 3500rpm was also impressive.

The result was a 143mph Capri with enough grunt to pull cleanly from 1000rpm and give a kick in the back higher up the rev range; 0-60mph was accomplished in just over 6secs. It was inevitably a keen oversteerer, but felt stable and surprisingly 'right'. Racing transmission from the Mustang and a Borg Warner limited slip diff kept the power down in a straight line, at least, and there

Capri in Australia............................

The other major export markets for the Capri were Australia and New Zealand. The Capri was offered from 1969 in 1600 and 1600GT guises, the latter attracting unique twin stripe treatment for the bonnet and flanks, a GT decal on the filler cap, special wheels (with optional whitewall tyres) and the bizarre fitment of bonnet pins! Capris were sold with the catchphrase 'The car that reshapes your life'.

The pins persisted in the 1970 line-up, which included the GT/V6, basically an Aussie Capri 3000GT with unique wheels, different stripes and matt black bonnet. The adverts blurted that this was 'The new shape of power for the '70s'. There were even rumours of an Australian V8 Capri. But despite its popularity, the Capri did not enjoy the same life span down under as it did in Europe.

CAPRI II IN DETAIL

By the end of 1973, when the original Capri was on its last legs, some of the shine had gone from this prodigal son of the Mustang. For sure, it had just broken the magic million production figure but its market share was waning fast. In Germany, sales had slumped from 3.5 per cent of the total market in its first year to just 1.5 per cent in 1973. In the healthy British market it was fairing a little better at 2.3 per cent, but even this was well down on the first year's 3 per cent share.

A revised model was called for. So was born project Diana, which would become the Capri II. In many ways it was a softer car than the first edition, larger, more practical and more comfortable. A pilot batch was made in December 1973 but production proper actually began in January 1974.

The wheelbase and front track were identical to that of the outgoing Capri but the rear track was increased by 2.2in. All the sheet metal was changed to create a slightly more bulky car: longer by 0.8in, wider by 2.1in and taller by almost 1in.

Project Diana was born to address the Capri's ageing problems. This rendering shows how the Capri was made smoother and larger, while retaining that essential family appearance.

At the bottom end of the scale, the base 1300 still made sense at a time when fuel prices were rocketing. Sales of the 1300 in Britain actually rose substantially during the mid-1970s.

The major news for the Capri II was the arrival of a hatchback, which made the new car extremely practical – indeed, more practical than many family cars, and untouched among coupés. From all angles, the new Capri looked very different. Big, rectangular headlamps, smaller bonnet bulge, dipping waist-line (to increase the glass area) and the loss of the hockey-stick side accent made it smoother, almost to the point of blandness.

The single most important change was the introduction of a hatchback. The idea of rear hatches was only just gaining currency in 1974, and the Capri was something of a coupé trail-blazer in this respect. It certainly made it much more practical, although some rigidity problems were encountered during development, necessitating extra metal to beef up the rear end. Of course that pushed weight up, and it also transpired that the aerodynamics were inferior to those of the Mk1.

Another major change was a big increase in the glass area, particularly the rear window and side glass, which now dipped around the waist. The rear three-quarter window was notably larger, and a convincing answer to critics of the Mk1's poor rear visibility. The windscreen remained the same as before.

Stylistically the Capri II was very recognisably an evolution of the 1969 original, but the hockey stick side mouldings were now absent, the door handles became flush-fitting and the fuel filler flap moved from the rear pillar to a new position on the wing.

Braking was improved, with new solid 9.75in front discs and thicker rear drums. Power steering, meanwhile, became an option for the first time on Capris. Suspension spring rates were softened considerably in keeping with

This Ford shot of a 3000 Ghia indulging in hooligan manoeuvres could easily have been an out-take from *The Professionals*. Step on it, Doyle.

the Capri's move towards a more family-oriented market.

The UK engine range remained the same as that for the post-September 1972 Capri Mk1, with one exception. The old Corsair overhead valve 1996cc V4 engine was superseded by the Pinto overhead cam 1993cc in-line engine, which had previously been fitted only in American-specification Capris. With an output of 98bhp, it was a solid performer: 108mph maximum and 0-60mph in 10.5secs.

The gearbox was a new close-ratio unit for all models except the 3000, which retained the Granada 'box it had gained in 1972. Final drives varied according to model, from 4.125:1 up to 3.09:1. Automatic transmission was now available for all Capris except the 1300, but it was now Ford's own C3 three-speed unit (replacing the old Borg Warner 35 'box).

New trim levels appeared for the revised range. The base version was the L, the XL added such items as a brake servo and heated rear window, the 1600GT had a more powerful engine, and both 1600GT and 2000GT received separate folding rear seats and four extra gauges.

A new top-of-the-range Ghia trim level appeared, having such extras as special alloy wheels, halogen headlamps, vinyl roof, tilt-and-slide sunroof, rear wash/wipe, headrests, tinted glass, push-button radio, body side rubbing strip, special 'Rialto' seat upholstery and different interior trim. Both Ghia models available in Britain (2000 and 3000) were mostly sourced from Cologne; only a few hundred were made at Halewood, the last ones in early 1976.

The instruments were carried over from the later 'Mk1½' Capris, although a panel light rheostat was now included. The large rear hatch was held up by gas struts and the rear seats – bench for lowly models, split

individual seats for GT and Ghia – folded flat. Rear wash/wipe was optional (standard on the Ghia), as was a cover for the boot area.

A new range of wheels appeared for the Capri II. The base models had new ventilated pressed steel disc wheels (still of 5in width), while spoked sports wheels were optional at first but soon standardised on GT and some higher specification models. The new Ghia models came with an attractive new design of 5½in spoked alloys.

The official launch occurred on 28 February 1974. The UK range extended from the base 1300L (£1731) up to the 3000 Ghia (£3109). The new Capri proved immediately popular: production across Europe reached 183,000 in the first year, although it began to tail away in successive years.

In March 1975 came the first and only Capri II special edition, the iconic 'Midnight' Capri, actually called simply Capri S. It was based on the 1600GT model, or optionally on the 2000GT or 3000GT, and featured all-black paintwork, blacked-out brightwork and black bumpers, topped off with gold coachlining, gold badges and gold finished alloy wheels. Even the interior brightwork was all epoxy powder coated black, the headlining was black and the seats had gold panels set in black cloth. Less well known is that a tiny batch of S models was despatched with white paint and white bumpers. The Capri S also featured tinted glass and harder springs. It went on sale in the UK in June 1975 at prices from £2330, and just over 2000 were made at Halewood.

A range-wide equipment hike in October 1975 made the Capri more appealing, and the range was rejigged at the same time. A new base 1300 model joined the 1300L, and could be distinguished by its plain steel wheels, black bumpers and window surrounds, non-reclining seats, single-piece rear seat and rubber boot mat. All models had a heated rear window, cloth seats and brake servo.

Split folding rear seats were a feature of more up-market Capri II models, such as this Ghia. Luggage capacity increased from 8.2 to 11.3cu ft, or an impressive 18.7cu ft with the rear seats folded flat. Interiors were kept very much as they were since the 1972 facelift. The new Ghia trim level was rather plush: standard headrests, radio and Rialto cloth upholstery.

L models gained standard sports wheels, cloth-covered reclining front seats, split rear seats and a door mirror. The XL name was dropped in favour of GL and given lots of extras: sports wheels, waist strip, rear wash/wipe, centre console, clock, GT type seats and halogen headlamps.

Also in October 1975, the S became a regular production offering, initially built in Britain but soon imported exclusively from Germany, replacing the GT models. Colours other than black were available, an add-on glass-fibre front spoiler was standard, as well as 5½in alloy wheels, a radio, inertia reel seat belts, striped seats and a three-spoke sports steering wheel. The 3000S also had standard power steering, as did the 3000 Ghia. At the top of the range, all Ghias were now fitted with a remote control door mirror.

From February 1976, the 1300 received a 50bhp 'economy' engine, by the simple expedient of fitting a Sonic Idle carburettor, a new type which added a sonic shock wave to the air stream to improve efficiency. Two months later, automatic transmission ceased to be offered on S models and the 3000 Ghia was listed as 'automatic standard, manual optional'.

A watershed year for the Capri came in 1976. The Halewood factory ceased to produce Capris after a run of eight years. Why? Capri volumes were decreasing and probably Ford already knew that the American market would soon be brought to an end, drastically reducing the output at Cologne. Economics suggested centralising production at Cologne, and so all production was transferred to Germany in the period from August to

October 1976. The last British Capri, chassis number 51574, rolled out of the factory in October 1976. Some 398,440 Capris, a substantially smaller volume than the German factory produced, had been built in Britain. Thereafter the vacant lines at the Halewood factory were used to increase Escort production instead.

There was one final sting in the Capri II tale. In August 1977, Ford launched a scheme called Series X which would, according to Ford, 'ensure that Ford owners are at the forefront of the customising scheme'. Kits were selected by Ford from the RS parts catalogue and sold as X packs, to be fitted by Ford dealers. Parts were variously sourced from Ford of Britain, Zakspeed and Ford AVO.

Naturally the X specification was intended mainly for the 3000S. The package comprised an engine upgrade to 175bhp and 194lb ft of torque, thanks to triple Weber carburettors, cast alloy manifolding, larger inlet and exhaust valves and an electric fuel pump. A Capri X like this could do 130mph and 0-60mph in 7.4secs.

Customers could also specify a limited slip differential, ventilated disc brakes with Granada calipers, 7½in four-spoke alloy wheels with 205/60 or 225/60 tyres, stiffened

The Midnight Hour – or March 1975, to be exact. Ford launches its JPS inspired colour scheme for the so-called Capri S. Colour-coded black bumpers and brightwork contrasted with gold wheels, coachlining and badges.

On 'Midnight' S models, even the interior was colour-coded black and gold. Yes, that really is gold cloth.

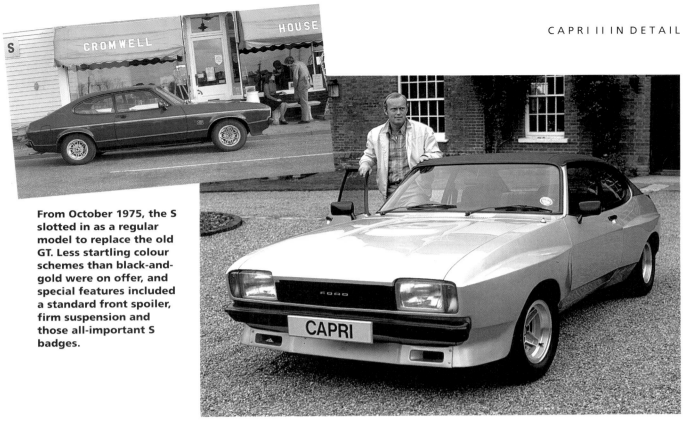

From October 1975, the S slotted in as a regular model to replace the old GT. Less startling colour schemes than black-and-gold were on offer, and special features included a standard front spoiler, firm suspension and those all-important S badges.

suspension, uprated front anti-roll bar and anti-dive kit, glass-fibre front and rear spoilers, and extremely wide 'Spa' glass-fibre wheelarch extensions from Zakspeed to cover those fat wheels. The whole caboodle would add no less than £2331 to the price of your Capri. Many of these components, particularly the cosmetic items, could be fitted to lesser Capris. X pack models remained available until 1980, by which time the Capri III was on stream.

Testers behind the wheel of the full-house 3000S X praised the performance but criticised the roughness and noise. They were enthusiastic about the firm handling and decent ride but not too keen about the sluggish and noisy limited slip diff. They liked the gearchange but not the brakes. Still, for an all-in price of £9625, it was certainly more exciting than the similarly priced Porsche 924 and Saab 900 Turbo.

By the time the Capri II was replaced in spring 1978, it had maintained its position in the British market as the best-selling coupé, and regularly appeared in the top ten best-seller lists. Overall, 404,169 Capri IIs were made.

Capri II in Germany..........................

Simultaneous with its launch in Britain, the Capri II went on sale in Germany and other continental markets with the advertising slogan 'A Clear Line of Reason'. With the Capri II, there was much greater harmonisation between

X-File: the ultimate Capri II offering arrived in 1977 under the name Series X. In Britain this consisted of packages taken from the RS parts catalogue, including major engine modifications, stiffer suspension, wide wheels and enormous glass-fibre wheel arches.

the Halewood and Cologne ranges. Now all engines were shared, with the exception of the faithful old 108bhp 2.3-litre V6, which remained unique to Germany and was offered in place of the overhead camshaft 2.0-litre.

There were other minor engine differences. The 1300 engine was now the same overhead valve Escort unit that had been fitted to British Capris since the very beginning, but it developed 2bhp less at 55bhp (and from August 1974 that dropped to 54bhp). There was also a low-compression version of the 1599cc overhead camshaft engine, developing 68bhp.

Only one German Capri, the 1300, had the new close-ratio gearbox specified on all UK Capris but for the 3000. Instead, the Taunus/Cortina 'box was used for the 1600 and 2300, with wider-spaced ratios. The 3000 stuck with the Consul/Granada gearbox. Sales of the 3000 reflected the oil crisis which was in full cry in 1974: a piffling 188 were sold in Germany that year.

The new Ghia trim option was produced principally in Cologne. On the continental market, it was available for 1600, 2300 and 3000 models; in Britain, the choice of

Fashions were changing in 1974, and this German publicity shot emphasises the more practical, family-orientated role which the Capri II fulfilled.

Ghias was 2000 or 3000. The 'Midnight' Capri S was launched in Germany too, initially as a 1000-off special edition, in April 1975.

In 1975 Capri production ended at the Saarlouis factory in the extreme west of Germany, as it geared up to produce the new Fiesta. Henceforth all German production would be concentrated at Cologne.

From May 1976, the 88bhp 1600GT engine was dropped in Germany and replaced by the familiar 90bhp 2.0-litre V6, which had been absent from the Capri for four years. This 2000 model was available in GL, S and Ghia trims and boasted standard gas-filled dampers.

A whole raft of improvements was introduced in May 1976. There were now three column stalks for lighting, wipers and indicators/horn, and intermittent wash/wipe. All Capris but for the base 1300 now had a heated rear window, L models gained individual folding rear seats (some time after UK model cars), S and Ghia models received a new design of 5.5in alloy wheel, and the S gained a front spoiler. Export Capri S models also had bumper overriders. One interesting aside was a Capri unique to the French and Italian markets – a 1300GT model which appealed in those countries because of their special taxation laws.

German production was very healthy in 1974 at 146,429 units, but it plunged the following year to just 78,826 as the oil crisis dug in and the European car market collapsed. After Halewood closed its doors to the Capri, production rose again to over 90,000 units in 1977

Capri IIs continued to be offered in Germany with different engines, notably the 2300 V6. The Ghia trim level which was produced mainly in Cologne was available on 1600, 2300 and 3000 models on the German market. From 1976, all Capri production transferred to Cologne. Clever brochure for Capri II had an opening tailgate for a front cover. Alongside is the German launch press pack.

but thereafter it was downhill all the way. Sales on the home market dropped from 25,164 in 1974 to 18,429 in 1977 but exports to Britain would keep the Cologne lines at a reasonable kilter for several years to come.

Capri II in America ....

No Capris were imported into America for the 1975 model year, as stocks of Capri Mk1s had to be cleared, so the Capri II arrived in the 'States in March 1975 as a (very early) '76 model.

The Capri continued in America, and was frankly a better car than the domestic Mustang II. This is a 2.8-litre model (right) with standard Rostyle wheels. American swansong (below): the R/S was the US equivalent of an X Pack. Such gaudy add-on packages did nothing to reverse the Capri's declining fortunes in the US, and the Capri II was withdrawn in 1977.

The advertising line went 'The new sexy European is everything the original was. And more'. And if you did not get the message, it summed up by saying the Capri II was 'sexier than ever'. The US version differed from its European cousin in its continued adoption of quad headlamps, black radiator grille with 'Capri' lettering in the centre, amber parking/signal lamps incorporated in the front and rear wings, and, of course, the oversized Federal bumpers front and rear which added no less than 6in (152mm) to the overall length.

A brand new engine was available for the Capri II, a 2.3-litre four-cylinder overhead camshaft unit not seen on any other Capri model. This was the last all-new engine to find its way under the Capri's bonnet and brought the total number of engines fitted to road-going production Capris world-wide up to a staggering 18. Naturally the Cologne 2.8-litre V6 continued to be offered too.

The range was a little bigger than before in America, with a choice of base, Ghia and S trim levels. The S model was available in black or white with gold striping and gold wheels. Once again, a decor group was an option, consisting of contoured rear seats, embossed vinyl trim, 'woodtone' instrument panel, opening rear quarter windows, carpets on the lower doors, exhaust tail-pipe trims and various minor extras.

Prices of the Capri II began at $4117. This was cheaper than imports like the Toyota Celica, VW Scirocco and Datsun 280Z, but it began to look rather costly compared with domestic products – a '76 Mustang II cost just $3525. Compared with the good old days of the Capri Mk1, sales began to take a dive.

The launch of a Le Cat Black S option group for 1977 did not halt the change in fortunes. This rather gaudy decor pack – which corresponded to European 'Midnight' S models – included such items as black-out chrome mouldings, extensive tape stripes, gold accents and a black-and-gold interior. Another dealer-fitted decor group was the Rally Cat pack: twin-striped bonnet and hatch (the latter with a spoiler fitted), plus large 'Capri' decals low on the doors.

The last year of Capri imports to the 'States was 1977. The official reasons were a strong Deutschmark and the imminent announcement of a new Mercury Capri, a badge-engineered version of the Mustang III that was launched in 1978. Unofficially, declining sales must have played a part in the decision.

Whatever the reason, the final German-built Capris were brought into America in August 1977, and the very last cars were sold during '78. Still, America had been a very important market for the Capri, and crucial to the dominance of Cologne among Ford's European production sites. No fewer than 464,729 Capris of all types were imported to the US over seven years – just over a third of all Capris made during that period. The loss of the American market severely dented Capri production in Germany.

CAPRI III IN DETAIL

The Capri III was born here: this is the 1976 Geneva Show concept called Modular Aerodynamic which showed the way for many of the wind-cheating measures adopted for the next generation Capri.

Although it was never officially described as the Capri III, the 1978 evolution of the Capri II is universally referred to as such. Ford themselves called the project Carla, a programme which was instituted in April 1977 and reached the market in less than a year, arriving in March 1978; pilot production actually began with a batch of 170 cars at the end of 1977. It is easy to surmise from this short lead time that the changes were not as far-reaching as the first make-over of 1974.

The fact that the Mk1 Capri was actually more aerodynamic than the Capri II had been a cause for concern. At the 1976 Geneva Motor Show, a 'concept' Capri called Modular Aerodynamic had been shown with front and rear spoilers, vaned grille, faired-in quad headlamps and flush wheel trims. This interesting and aerodynamically efficient 'droop-snoot' Capri proved to be the basis for much of the work that went into making the Capri III a more slippery and efficient shape.

Hence all Capri III models would get an integral front spoiler, and most would also have an Escort RS2000 style rear spoiler. Ford claimed a drag coefficient figure of 0.403 for Capri III (compared with 0.428 for Capri II), but on S models the Cd dropped to 0.374.

Perhaps the main distinguishing feature of the Capri III was its new nose, in particular its quad headlamps; no Capri II model – apart from American ones – had four headlamps. These were a purely marketing-led development but the quad lights co-incidentally improved aerodynamics, as a new smoother bonnet and wing shape partially hooded them. The bonnet bulge was also made slimmer and the grille became Ford's corporate plastic aerofoil louvre type.

A laminated windscreen was standardised across the range, and most versions now had a rear parcel shelf which lifted with the tailgate. The rear light clusters were enlarged and contained ridges to keep them visible even when dirty. All models except S versions received black rubber side strips on their lower flanks, the S having coloured, graded side stripes on the same level as the wrap-around black moulded bumpers, front and rear. Since the square headlamps had been replaced, the front indicators had to be repositioned in the bumper.

Inside, things remained much as before, but virtually all models now had the smaller 14in diameter RS2600 style AVO three-spoke steering wheel (the 3000 Ghia kept the old two-spoke wheel), new trim colours, a satin finish for the fascia and some extra padding on the dash. Recaro seats with mesh-filled head restraints became an option for S models.

As far as engines were concerned, things remained very much as before. Only the 1300 engine changed, reverting to its pre-Sonic Idle carburettor 57bhp specification; there was a 73bhp tuned version called GT

The main aerodynamic changes for the 1978 Capri III were a four-headlamp nose across the range, reshaped hooded bonnet, front spoiler and vaned grille. The quoted drag coefficient dropped from 0.428 to 0.403, or even less on S models. At the rear, all Capris got larger light clusters with ridges in the lenses.

The full trim level range at 1978 launch was, in descending order, Ghia (left), S (foreground), GL (centre) and L (right).

Inside things remained largely unchanged, except for the adoption of an RS style three-spoke steering wheel and a satin finish for the fascia.

or Sport in some markets, but not the UK, and there was no Capri III 1300 model in Germany. In the UK, the rest of the range comprised 1600 engines in 72bhp and 88bhp states of tune, the familiar 98bhp 2000 in-line four and the 138bhp 3000 V6. In Germany, there was no 88bhp 1600S model, but customers could choose a low-compression 68bhp 1600 model as well as the standard 72bhp version. Continental markets also had the option of two further V6 engines – the 90bhp 2.0-litre V6 and 108bhp 2.3-litre V6.

Suspension was kept much the same but gas–filled Bilstein dampers were now standard on all but the very basic models, and sportier ones had thicker anti-roll bars.

Previous Capris relied on 6000-mile major service intervals, but Ford made great play of the extended 12,000-mile intervals for Capri III – although some aspects of 3.0-litre cars still required more frequent attention. Self-adjusting brakes and lubrication for life for the gearbox, rear axle and steering all played their part.

Thanks to improved aerodynamics and carburation, both performance and economy were better. Even the base 1300 reached 89mph, while the 3000 was quoted as having a 0-60mph time of 8.5secs.

Sales of the revised Capri began in March 1978. In Germany the adverts proclaimed: 'Luckily, it's no dream car', while in Britain the ad copy told us the new Capri was 'The difference between driving and just motoring'.

Since the Zakspeed racing operation was about to go into top gear in Group 5 racing, Ford saw a good opportunity to market its X pack merchandise on the back of this success. The UK market modifications are described in the chapter on the Capri II (see pages 42-43), but it is worth mentioning the German homologated RS extras here. These included the Zakspeed glass-fibre arches and spoilers, wider alloy wheels and so on, but some unique but rather mild engine tweaks were also available: a tuning kit for the 3000 that gave an extra 7bhp (up to 145bhp), and another for the two 1600 types that boosted power from 68bhp to 80bhp (low compression) or from 72bhp to 88bhp (high compression).

Production changes..........................

The rapid development of Project Carla meant that there were still some creases to iron out in the launch range. Very quickly, the base 1300 model was dropped in the UK (leaving just a 1300L model) and some equipment changes occurred in August 1978: L models at last were fitted with a radio, the S gained rear fog lamps and the Ghia received an upgraded radio/cassette player. In April 1979 came more minor improvements: head restraints and two door mirrors (the driver's side remote-operated) for the GL; extra sound-proofing and a remote driver's door mirror for the S; twin mirrors, a sports steering wheel and headlamp washers for the Ghia.

Over the last months of 1979 and the early months of 1980, a viscous coupled fan for all Capris raised quoted power outputs fractionally. The 1300 engine was up 3bhp to 60bhp, the 1600 went up to 73bhp (or 91bhp in healthier S tune), and the 2000 rose by 3bhp to 101bhp. There was also, very briefly and for certain markets only, a low-compression 1600 unit in 1980 developing 70bhp. For continental customers, the 2300 models gained a useful boost in power, up 6bhp to 114bhp, thanks to a higher (9.0:1) compression ratio and larger valves, ports and inlets.

In February 1980, at the same time as the 1600S was dropped, the first of a whole string of special edition Capris hit the market. This was the GT4, a 1600L with extra instruments, twin coachlines and a bonnet decal; it sold for £4375 in the UK. The same edition had been marketed in Germany three months earlier.

But something far more interesting was on the horizon. A Ford development department called Special Vehicle Engineering (SVE) was set up in April 1980 at Dunton, Essex, specifically to engineer niche products in the Ford line-up. These would eventually include such performance legends as the XR3i, Escort Turbo and Sierra Cosworth.

However, SVE's very first project was the installation of a fuel-injected version of the 2.8-litre 'Cologne' V6 into the Capri. Actually such an installation had already been tried by a team of Ford Motorsport engineers at Cologne as early as 1978, and the prototype was even driven by some journalists. The 2.8-litre V6 engine would replace the ageing 3.0-litre 'Essex' V6, which had already been superseded in the Granada and was looking out of date from the points of view of emissions and production logistics.

The 'Cologne' V6 was a 60-degree overhead valve design that had been developed as early as 1974 for use in the Ford Mustang and US-specification Capri, although not with fuel injection. The injection system was the seminal Bosch K-Jetronic set-up, except for some export markets which received different Bosch injection. Capri differences compared with the Granada installation included slight modifications to improve reliability at high revs and, on the cooling side, the addition of an oil/water heat exchanger, viscous-coupled fan and high-density US-specification radiator; there was also a new large-bore, twin-pipe exhaust system. Despite these tweaks, quoted power output of 160bhp was initially the same as for the Granada, although the Granada figure would later be adjusted to a (presumably more accurate) 150bhp.

Performance claims for the new Capri 2.8i were up on the outgoing 3000: top speed was quoted at 130mph (210kph), with 0-60mph coming up in 7.8secs. Officially this Capri was said to be the most powerful production car ever built by Ford of Europe.

To cope with the increased power, the brakes were upgraded, with ventilated 9.76in (248mm) discs up front. New brake pad and lining materials improved feel and fade, while a new 'G-valve' apportioned braking load. Bilstein dampers were retained but the springs were toughened up front and rear, and now only single-leaf springs were used at the back. Officially, ride height was 1in lower for the 2.8i. Naturally, there was power steering and new wheels in the form of 7×13in Wolfrace Sonic alloy wheels (thickened up by SVE) fitted with 205/60 VR13 tyres.

The overall effect of the mechanical improvements was a much more sophisticated machine. The fuel injection removed much of the old 3.0-litre Capri's

The X Pack option remained available for Series III Capris. Here a fully specified 3.0 X sits appropriately alongside Gordon Spice's Group 1 championship winning car at Thruxton.

In Germany the equivalent of the X Pack was the 3.0 RS. Here is a batch of RS equipped cars with 145bhp engines and Ford Rallye Sport colour schemes.

agricultural feel, and the car was faster too. The suspension now worked much more effectively, combining with those fat, low-profile tyres to transform the big Capri's handling from brutish to sharp and endlessly entertaining. The only demerit was perhaps a less all-encompassing torque band.

To celebrate its new-found sophistication, the 2.8i was treated to some minor cosmetic changes too: twin coachlines, 'injection' wording on the front wings and rear hatch, colour-coded door mirrors and the option of metallic and two-tone paint schemes.

Inside, the new 2.8i became the most luxurious Capri yet seen. Its Recaro seats were given crushed velour edging, and their 'Carla' tartan trim was echoed in the door panels. Standard equipment included a push-button stereo radio/cassette and a tilt-and-slide steel sunroof.

The 2.8i was first produced in Germany in February 1981 for a March launch at the Geneva Motor Show. It cost DM25,950, some DM3820 more than the outgoing 3000 Ghia. Britain had to wait for the 2.8i until June 1981, when it was catalogued at £7995. World-wide 2.8i sales kicked off at an encouraging 5500 annually.

One month later, in July 1981, an even more special Capri was launched, although its market was restricted to Germany and Switzerland. This was the 2.8 Turbo, the ultimate road-going production line Capri. There was no injection equipment on the Turbo, as it used the standard Granada carburettor engine – with single twin-choke Solex – as its basis. These engines were bedecked with RS badging, reflecting the 2.8 Turbo's sales outlets.

Famed turbo expert Michael May, who had built his first Capri turbo in 1969, did most of the conversion work, using a Garrett turbo instead of his favoured KKK. May's efforts produced an engine with 188bhp at 5500rpm, and torque also shot up to 194lb ft at 4500rpm. That was sufficient for a top speed of 137mph (220kph) and a 0-60mph time of well under 8secs.

The 2.8 Turbo's bodywork modifications were developed and manufactured by Zakspeed at its Niederzissen plant. All the new panels were made of glass-fibre. The subtly but noticeably widened front and rear wings were basically X Pack specification, but the very deep front spoiler and matt black deformable triple-pylon rear aerofoil were all-new. 'Turbo' decals on the bonnet, boot and doors announced you were driving something special. Cars were usually supplied in plain white, to be dolled up by dealers or customers as required.

Also standard were AVO spoked alloy wheels (6.5in or 7in width) with wide 235/60 VR13 tyres, and a limited slip diff was an option. Inside, the interior benefited from special seats and a four-spoke steering wheel, although surprisingly there was no turbo boost gauge.

The 2.8 Turbo was built by Ford RS Operations and sold through Ford RS dealers at a cost at launch of DM33,300, some DM6150 more than a 2.8i. Local publicity gushed: 'Technical sharpness. Perfection. Reliability. Styling. Comfort. Individuality'; and it played heavily on the connection between the road car and the all-conquering Zakspeed Turbo racers. The Turbo lasted only one year, being withdrawn in September 1982 after a run of just 200 cars, all of them left-hand drive.

There were other deaths in the Capri range at this

time. The 1300 models, which had not been offered at all in Germany in Capri III form but had soldiered on in Britain, finally fluttered out of production at the beginning of 1982. The 1600 was retired in Germany in 1983 after a final run of rather feeble striped 1600GT models, although the 1600 kept going for British customers until the bitter end. Another casualty in 1981 was the German 2.0-litre V6 engine, which had been going since 1969.

One minor birth in January 1981 was the 1600LS, which effectively plugged a gap caused by the demise of the 1600S one year previously. It echoed the old S in its sports wheels and 185 tyres, trim and suspension, but all this was mere face-paint since the car kept the less powerful 1600 engine.

Special editions now became a prime method of raising the profile of the now familiar Capri, thereby selling more units. A whole string of them flowed in the early 1980s. No fewer than three were launched in just one month (July 1981): the Calypso, Cameo and Tempo. The two-tone Calypso (at £5120) was based on the 1600LS; the Cameo and Tempo (from £3995) were based on the 1300L or 1600L and slotted in as budget models with no body side mouldings or centre console.

Then came the Cabaret in May 1982, based on L

specification but with a 1600 or 2000 engine; it had two-tone paint, a sunroof, sports wheels, Ghia centre console, extra gauges and tinted glass. A Cabaret II edition followed in December 1982, by which time there had also been a Calypso II.

From 1982, the Capri range was severely pared down even in the UK, its best market. As well as all 1300 models, the 1600L and 1600GL were dropped, leaving the 1600LS as the only 1600 model. Likewise, the 2000GL and 2000 Ghia were dropped and only the 2000S remained. The 3000 models, of course, had been replaced by the 2.8i in 1981.

Meanwhile, the remaining Capri range received a dose of development. A raft of improvements was announced at the October 1982 Motor Show, although they did not reach the showrooms until January 1983. The old four-speed gearbox was replaced by a more suitable five-speeder from the Granada; only the 1600 retained the old four-speed 'box, and even then five speeds became an option. There were two types of five-

A new lease of life was bestowed on the Capri when Ford SVE engineers fitted a fuel-injected 2.8-litre Cologne V6 into the engine bay. The new 2.8 Injection suddenly turned the Capri into one of the great performance bargains. Main cosmetic change was Wolfrace Sonic alloy wheels. Testers praised the urge and smoothness of the new 2.8i 160bhp engine, while tougher springing and fat low profile tyres transformed the car's handling.

The most spectacular full production Capri was undoubtedly the 2.8 Turbo produced in Germany for one year only (1981-82). Fat arches, big front and rear spoilers, Turbo decals and wide wheels hinted at the 188bhp Garrett turbocharged engine and 137mph top speed. Only 200 were built. Even Her Majesty's police forces (left) were not blind to the 2.8-litre Capri's charms as a pursuit vehicle.

The Laser became a production model from 1984 when it joined the 2.8i as the sole survivor in the UK Capri range. Both 1600 and 2000 versions of the Laser were marketed.

speed 'box. Four-cylinder cars (and the German 2.3-litre V6) simply gained an extra overdrive gear; in other respects the internals of the 'box were retained. By contrast, the new 2.8i five-speed 'box had notably higher internal ratios, allowing much more comfortable cruising and reduced noise levels, at the cost of some loss in gearchange smoothness. Fuel consumption was also notably improved. Axle ratios were, however, kept as before, varying according to model: from 3.77:1 for the 1600 to 3.09:1 for the 2.8i.

Several minor specification changes were made at the same time. To celebrate the switch to five gears, Capris received a Granada gear knob, opening rear quarter windows became standard, and the old tartan Carla interior trim switched to Monza grey cloth.

The end of Capri sales on the continent came in 1984, and a number of special editions were launched to mark the occasion. The first was the Laser of January 1984, based on the 1600. From April 1984, there was also a run-out edition of so-called 'Super' models: the Super GT in 2000 and 2300 guises and the 2.8 Super Injection, which had larger alloy wheels and extra colour-coding; this version would remain as a production model for the UK as the 2.8 Injection Special.

The UK also saw the Laser special edition in June 1984, priced at £5990 in 1600 form and £6371 with a 2000 engine. Lasers boasted colour-coded grille, headlamp surrounds and door mirrors, together with tinted glass, four-spoke alloy wheels with 185/70 tyres, 'Laser' side stripe motifs, a leather gear knob, radio/cassette, full instrument panel and new cloth trim. Lasers with a 2000 engine received a five-speed gearbox as standard (optional on the 1600), or optional automatic. For British customers Lasers ran on as replacements for the 1600LS and 2000S – indeed they were the only Capri models available other than the 2.8i – right up until 1987. Late Capris all had a six-year anti-corrosion warranty.

By 1984, the UK was the only market in which the Capri was selling in worthwhile numbers. Indeed it was still in the Top Twenty best-seller lists, having shifted 22,254 examples in 1983. As such, Ford decided to end left-hand drive production and axe the Capri in continental markets. As of November 1984, all Capri production became right-hand drive only. Hence 1984 marked the end of the line for all uniquely continental market Capris, such as the 2.3-litre V6.

Some turbo Capris

The Capri's position in Britain had received a boost in October 1982, when Aston Martin Tickford showed a specially modified Capri at the Birmingham Motor Show. Tickford was a famous coachbuilding name that had been taken over by Aston Martin, and the so-called Tickford Capri was therefore viewed as a prestige product.

It came about after a fortuitous meeting in October 1981 between Bob Lutz (Ford of Europe chairman), Victor Gauntlett (Aston Martin chairman) and Capri racer and journalist John Miles. At one stage it looked like the car would become a regular production Ford, but in the end Lutz was transferred back to America and the project was relegated to the back burner. Ultimately Ford's involvement was merely semi-official: although Aston Martin developed the mechanicals itself, SVE at Dunton provided technical assistance, and Ford would eventually offer the car through selected dealers.

The Tickford Capri 2.8T was enhanced in almost every area. Most important was the addition of a turbocharger. Michael May's conversion for the German 2.8 Turbo was considered but rejected because the turbo would have needed relocation to suit right-hand drive. In the end the team selected an IHI turbocharger and Garrett intercooler for the 2.8i engine, mounted on a special manifold. Also new was AFT digital electronic ignition and special tuning, while the Bosch fuel injection system was retained intact. The result was an engine

Aston Martin's Tickford wing made quite a serious car out of the Capri in 1982 when it showed the 2.8T. Aerodynamics were a major part of the package: note the flush wheel trims, blanked-off grille, deep spoiler and side skirts.

developing a massive 205bhp at 5500rpm and an even more impressive 260lb ft of torque at just 3500rpm.

Other mechanical changes included extra lubrication for the five-speed gearbox and, more significantly, a heavily revised rear end. The rear axle was located by an A-frame and the rear springs had spacers in them. There was also an optional limited slip differential before the 2.8i adopted such a set-up, and the steel diff casing was replaced by a finned aluminium cover. Equally important, the rear drums were replaced with 10.43in solid discs. Everyone agreed that the new running gear was a significant improvement over the archaic Capri's set-up.

Aerodynamics were aided by a Simon Saunders designed glass-fibre body kit, which reduced the Cd to 0.37 and cut front and rear end lift by 40 per cent. The body kit consisted of a blanked-off grille, deep front bumper/spoiler with a letterbox air intake, chiselled side skirts, ground-effect style rear bumper/valance and an enlarged boot spoiler. Unlike production cars, the prototype also had flush wheel trims and an undertray.

Inside, the standard Capri 2.8i interior was retained, although it gained walnut veneer on the dash, leather trim, a curious triangular steering wheel boss, electric windows and an alarm system. Options included a full leather interior, Wilton carpeting, Pirelli P7 tyres and a stainless steel exhaust system.

The whole thing cost a substantial £14,985 (at a time when the standard 2.8i was £8125). But then you did get whopping performance: 140mph top speed, 0-60mph in a claimed 6.0secs and impressive in-gear acceleration. The press was extremely enthusiastic about the Tickford, particularly its raw speed. However, the all-or-nothing turbo boost and considerable turbo lag were criticised, and made fast cornering a matter of some skill – which was a shame because the revised rear end worked so well.

Tickford sold exactly 100 examples between the start of production in 1983 and the Capri's demise, the last Tickford being built in spring 1987. Examples are very much sought-after today.

Another semi-official turbocharged Capri came from Janspeed. They had offered a turbo kit for the 2.8i since 1983 but their ultimate offering was the phenomenal SS Turbo Capri sold through Ford dealers Currie Motors from 1985. It was fitted with the new 2.9-litre Cologne V6 with six-port head and turbo unit – maximum speed 165mph, 0-60mph in 5.7secs! But then it did cost £18,495...

In July 1986, Ford also officially approved a conversion by Turbo Technics for the Capri 2.8i. The addition of a Garrett T3 turbocharger and intercooler (for a reasonable £1395 plus tax) boosted power to between 200bhp and 230bhp depending on specification, and increased top speed to around 150mph. About 500 TT conversions were sold altogether, including earlier and less powerful versions.

Capri twilight ....

The closing chapters of the long-running Capri story begin in April 1984. This was the German launch date of the 2.8 Super Injection. It gained attractive lockable seven-spoke RS alloy wheels, standard Salisbury limited slip diff, body-colour grille and headlamp surrounds, and leather trim for the edges of the Recaro seats, steering wheel, gear knob and door panels.

This uprated 2.8i arrived in the UK in September 1984 as the 2.8 Injection Special, replacing the old 2.8i. Within two months, left-hand drive Capri production ended and the UK became the sole destination for the Injection Special.

The 2.8-litre Capri carried on to the bitter end, accompanied by the still-popular 1600 Laser and 2000 Laser. Naturally sales in the UK declined in the final years: 22,254 in 1983, 16,328 in 1984, 11,075 in 1985. But even at the very end the Capri maintained its clientele of enthusiastic purchasers who recognised a

Heart of the Tickford 2.8T was the turbocharged engine using an IHI turbo and Garrett intercooler. AFT electronic ignition and fine tuning helped it develop 205bhp, enough for a claimed 140mph and 0-60mph in 6.0secs.

Here is one reason why the 2.8T cost nearly £15,000. A walnut dash, special steering wheel, electric windows and alarm were standard, while full leather upholstery was optional.

Surely the most expensive Capri ever was this 1985 Currie Motors SS Turbo conversion. Customers got a claimed 165mph out of it but had to stump up £18,495 for the pleasure.

striking performance bargain when they saw one.

The Cologne plant ceased making Capris in December 1986 with a run of limited edition cars. It had been intended to make a final batch of 500 special Capris, but in the event the total number ran to 1038, arriving in Britain in spring 1987.

This limited edition run-out was called the 280, also commonly referred to as the 'Brooklands' because of its Brooklands metallic green paint scheme. This colour scheme extended to the front grille, headlamp surrounds and door mirrors, while the red-and-white coachlines incorporated a 'Capri 280' logo on the front wings and boot lid. The RS alloy wheels grew from 13in diameter to 15in, still of the same 7in width but shod with narrower 195/50 tyres.

Inside, the 280 got the full leather treatment: grey seats

with burgundy piping, plus matching gear knob and steering wheel rim. In all other respects, it was identical to the 2.8i Special. The price was a not inconsiderable £11,999, but all of the 1038 Capri 280s made were quickly snapped up.

The very last Capri 280 – and the very last Capri of all – rolled off the production line on 19 December 1986. However, this was *not* the final chassis number; that accolade went to a car finished on 18 December and punted out at a special ceremony at the Cologne plant. The air was rich with the smell of garlands and the scene

Seven-spoke alloys, a body-coloured grille, leather-edged seats and limited slip diff became standard from 1984 with the 2.8 Injection Special (above). In Germany this model was known as the Super Injection, and was the last Capri sold there. The very last of the Capris was the limited edition 280 (right), also called the Brooklands because of its green paintwork: 15in diameter alloy wheels, 195 section tyres and '280' decals were the major exterior distinguishing features.

was permeated with roof-mounted plaques reading 'Bye Bye Capri'. Notably, all of the media interest – a few motoring journalists and a BBC TV crew – was British, a situation which reflected the loyalty of the UK market to what had become a social icon. The death of the Capri even made the front cover of *Autocar* magazine, and journalist Mike McCarthy – an enthusiastic owner of a 280 – helped build the very last example off the line.

The final chassis number was GG 11896 J, the ultimate example of a long line of Capris stretching back over 18 years. Very large white Fablon numbers at the end of the production line stated with erroneous certainty that 1,886,647 Capris had been built in that time. The tally was later revised to more than 1.92 million examples. Not bad for any car, let alone one with a sporting image.

Plush interior treatment for the 280 included full leather seats with burgundy piping and matching leather gear knob and steering wheel. Only 1038 such cars were built at a cost of just under £12,000 each. Today they are prized examples of the Capri breed.

CAPRI IN COMPETITION

While it does boast a long and sometimes spectacularly impressive competition career, the main problem with the Capri in the great scheme of things was that it was a victim of poor timing. It arrived one year after the Escort, whose shining successes always seemed to put the Capri in the shade.

Ford also did not really have a pan-European competition policy. While there was plenty of co-operation between the two main wings of Ford's European operation, Ford of Great Britain and Ford of Germany, it never amounted to a unified approach. Each operation entered its own events and, since each used entirely different ranges of engines, the preparation was different in each country. However, racing engines were always developed and often produced in Britain, but more and more the Germans assumed control of their own competition effort. In the end, it was Cologne that dominated the Capri's competition career.

This was mainly because Ford of Great Britain saw no great benefit in racing the Capri. It went rallycrossing because the TV cameras were there; televised support for tarmac racing was, in the Capri years, frankly pathetic in Britain. The reverse was true on the continent, and there was great publicity to be gained from contesting, for

The Capri's first ever outing – and its first win – came just three days after the car was launched. Roger Clark drove this four-wheel drive rallycross Capri to victory at Croft in February 1969. British works racing Capri activity promptly ceased for almost two years.

instance, the European Touring Car Championship.

Just as the Escort had done one year earlier, near its launch in 1968, the Capri would be destined to win its very first competitive outing just days after the official launch of the road car. Ford was naturally extremely keen to glean maximum benefit from this very public display of success. The date was 8 February 1969, the venue the Croft rallycross circuit in the north of England. In front of an audience of millions watching the event on ITV's *World of Sport*, no less a figure than Roger Clark battled through to score first blood for the Capri.

Considering the short space of time for preparation and the inherent problems of the Capri as a race car, this was a satisfying achievement. The Capri was much heavier than the Escort and the BDA Twin Cam engine which was so effective in the Escort proved not to be so in the Capri. It will be remembered that the press tried a batch of pre-production Capris with BDA 16-valve engines

Three Capris competed in the 1970-71 rallycross championship, and Roger Clark – pictured here at Cadwell Park in 1971 – won with this 252bhp four-wheel drive car. Note the crude bonnet bulge to clear the Lucas fuel injection. These Capris were notoriously difficult to handle.

fitted at the Cyprus launch of the car, but these were to be the last Capris so powered.

Instead, Ford's competitions department concentrated on the 3.0-litre 'Essex' V6 engine which had already been established as a future fitting for road car use. It was easily tuneable, and Weslake had little trouble in porting the cylinder heads and reprofiling the camshaft to extract 160bhp. But it was rather too torquey for the nose-heavy Capri, whose traction ability was certainly in question on the rough stuff of rallycross circuits.

Therefore the radical decision was taken to make the Capri four-wheel drive. A Capri was despatched to Harry Ferguson Research Ltd of Coventry, the leading four-wheel drive specialists, and duly converted. Ferguson had some experience with engineering all-wheel drive V6 Ford Zodiacs for the police force, so this company was the natural choice.

There was a tremendous amount of work to do to effect the four-wheel drive conversion. In order to liberate space for the new transmission, parts of the front bulkhead and floorpan had to be hacked away, and the front chassis rails were chopped to make way for new front driveshafts. A new front subframe and new engine mounts were then fitted, and different suspension uprights – taken from the front-wheel drive Ford Taunus – were grafted into the metalwork.

Ferguson's components consisted of a new cast aluminium front differential and sump assembly. A new bell-housing was required to join the V6 engine and the ZF five-speed gearbox, and, remarkably, the centre differential was bolted directly to the back of the gearbox. From there, one shaft ran forwards to the front differential and one to the back axle.

At least one car was fitted with automatic transmission, which seems odd for a competition car. Another aborted experiment was Dunlop Maxaret anti-lock braking, but again the drivers did not favour this system in a competitive role and it was abandoned.

Roger Clark's Croft victory in the four-wheel drive Capri was so encouraging that Ford ordered further four-wheel drive cars to be converted by Ferguson in February 1969, but in the event the Capri race programme was mothballed, partly because the 3.0-litre engine had not yet appeared in the showrooms and partly because the UK-based competitions department was busy on the World Cup Rally effort with the Escort.

In fact, it would be almost two years before the Capri took to the rallycross scene again, in the 1970-71 season. This time the Capri was a much more ferocious animal, and the competitions effort was more serious. Roger Clark was retained as the main driver, with his brother Stan and Rod Chapman driving a further two cars. The 3.0-litre engine was given the treatment by Weslake once more, now being fitted with continuous port injection, larger inlet and exhaust valves, and an uprated camshaft, with the result that output increased to 220bhp.

At the end of 1970, Ford's number one driver, Roger Clark, was given a little edge when his Capri was treated to a clever new engine. The 3.0-litre V6 was bored out to 3.1 litres, fitted with a Len Bailey-designed aluminium cylinder head, and fed by Lucas mechanical fuel injection which sprouted up through the bonnet. Together with even bigger valves, the output now shot up to 252bhp.

The suspension on all three rallycross cars was beefed up with an extra leaf spring on either side at the rear, Bilstein dampers and harder bushes. Brakes were the normal disc/drum set-up, though with harder Ferodo pads and linings. Minilite wheels of 6×13in or 7×13in size were fitted with Dunlop tyres. Finally, a ZF five-speed gearbox was bolted to the Ferguson centre differential.

Four-wheel drive Capris were reputedly a handful to drive well. When they were piloted by an experienced pair of hands, they were very useful, as their successes would show. But a slight error coming into a corner meant the driver had to fight terminal understeer.

Ford threw occasional pro-celebrity FordSport days as a bit of fun, attracting such contenders as Frank Williams and Dave Brodie. This is a shot from the May 1970 meeting at Brands. The Capri's European rally debut (below) came in 1969. In the prestigious Tour de France, Jean François Piot piloted this 2300GT to a creditable sixth place, taking a class win.

There were two series in the 1970-71 rallycross season, at Cadwell Park and at Lydden. Both were televised, by ITV and BBC respectively. The Capris' main successes were scored in the Cadwell Park six-round series, where they rarely had a time handicap compared with the Hillman Imps and four-wheel drive Minis; as a result, they scored a straight 1-2-3 victory on points. At Lydden Hill, they often struggled to overcome 10sec penalties and driveshaft problems. It was certainly spectacular viewing, with mud flying everywhere, and the Capris looking like monsters alongside the Minis.

In Britain, Ford took much less of an interest in non-televised tarmac racing. Capris were supplied in occasional races on FordSport days, driven by celebrities and managers. These even included such luminaries as Frank Williams and Emerson Fittipaldi.

However, when a new Group 1 class was created for production saloon cars in 1972, there was an obvious chance for the 3.0-litre Capri to be competitive in privateer hands. Ford supplied a couple of cars for the season, driven by Dave Brodie and Dave Matthews, and they had 160bhp engines modified by Broadspeed or Racing Services. Despite some individual victories, however, the cars made no impression on the title fight.

While British Capris went mud-plugging, their counterparts in Cologne were taking a more serious stab

For the 1970 season, Ford launched an assault on the European Touring Car championship. The team was not really prepared for such a challenge, and Dieter Glemser's second place at the Tourist Trophy at Silverstone was Ford's best result. The championship went to Alfa Romeo that year.

at tarmac rallying. Ex-racer Jochen Neerpasch had become, at the age of just 28, head of Ford's competitions department within the Niehl complex at Cologne, and he masterminded Ford's racing programme with the Capri, with Mike Kranefuss as his deputy.

The model chosen for the job was the 2300GT, which at the outset in 1969 was the most powerful German-built Capri made, although still in prototype form and hence unhomologated. The 2300 engine was modified by Weslake, having triple carburettors and a high compression ratio, and boasted 170bhp. Lightly flared wheel arches allowed 7J rear and 6J front wheels to be fitted, while bumpers were deleted and Bilstein gas-filled dampers were installed.

The rallying 2300GT's first outing was in the Rallye Internationale Lyon/Charbonnières in March 1969, and an encouraging start it proved to be. Germans Dieter Glemser and Klaus Kaiser finished fourth in one car, while French driver Jean-François Piot and co-driver (and later Ferrari Formula 1 team manager) Jean Todt

The Capri had a much better ETC season in 1971, partly due to the homologation of the RS2600 for racing. Dieter Glemser was the star of the year, clinching the driver's title. Here he is (below) on his way to winning the Spa 24 Hours, one of his five ETC victories that year. Gerry Birrell (left) was another tireless Capri driver in the 1971 ETC championship; this is his appearance in the Jackie Stewart Tribute event in 1971.

took seventh. Glemser and Piot returned in August with Tim Schenken to compete in the Marathon de la Route 84-hour event, but were forced to retire.

There was better luck in the prestigious 1969 Tour de France, perhaps thanks to a hike in power, to 190bhp, courtesy of some more Weslake modifications and Lucas fuel injection. Three cars were entered but only one finished, that of Piot/Todt, in a creditable sixth place overall and first in class. The German 2.6-litre V6 engine arrived in time for a first outing at the Tour de Corse (Corsica) in November 1969. With 192bhp from the fuel-injected unit, Piot/Todt came home third overall in this gruelling event.

Grand plans were already afoot for the 1970 season, including a full assault on the European Touring Car Championship and a stab at the East African Safari. In the event, the latter programme would run into disastrous difficulties. That Safari would turn out to be a graveyard for most entrants, and the Capri team in particular.

Three cars were sent to Uganda for the start, with the following driver/co-driver combinations: Rauno Aaltonen/Peter Huth, Robin Hillyar/Jock Aird and Dieter Glemser/Klaus Kaiser. Ford were buoyed with confidence since Hillyar had won the 1969 Safari in a Taunus 20M. Everyone expected the lighter and faster Capri to do even better (it had 190bhp, after all), but reliability problems struck almost from the very beginning. The Kügelfischer fuel injection system which had been substituted for the previous Lucas system had problems coping with the high altitudes. Although he was leading in the early stages, Aaltonen retired after his car

Capris were absolutely dominant in 1972 ETC racing, Jochen Mass winning the title. Many celebrity drivers raced Capris that year too, such as Jackie Stewart and François Cevert, who were amazingly beaten by the British prepared John Miles/Brian Muir 3.0-litre Capri – seen in action here at Silverstone against two works RS2600s – in the Paul Ricard Six Hours in September. A surprise title came in 1972 when Timo Makinen (below) won the Finnish ice racing championship.

suffered main bearing failure. Hillyar's car broke a leaf spring, a valve spring and a cam follower, and then retired with a mud-filled clutch. Glemser's Capri ducked out after a broken prop shaft brought him to a halt.

It was not a good start to the 1970 season. Moreover, the amount of time devoted to the Safari left the Capri short on development and testing for the important European Touring Car (ETC) series and this would prove fateful as reliability problems set in. By comparison with the road and rally Capri, the track cars had extended wheel arches (to cover much wider split-rim wheels),

Thomas Ammerschlager was responsible for the new shape of the 1973 ETC Capri: squared-off arch extensions, bigger front spoiler and a slot in the rear wings to aid cooling. Gerry Birrell sits in the cockpit in this shot, although his tragic death scotched plans for him to race that year.

The 1973 race engine was bored out to nearly 3.0 litres and developed over 320bhp. Kügelfischer mechanical fuel injection and aluminium head are clearly visible. Also new for 1973 was clever under-bonnet ducting, which went a long way to boosting available power.

small front spoilers, and uprated suspension and brakes.

Again the 2300GT formed the basis of the 1970 ETC programme. However, the engine was bored out to 2397cc, given one of Weslake's aluminium cylinder heads and a higher compression ratio. Significantly, the UK-made Lucas injection system was abandoned in favour of Kügelfischer mechanical injection from Germany, as with the rally programme. Ford said that its engine developed 230bhp, although the true figure was probably a lot less.

The ETC season began unpromisingly at Monza. Here Manfred Mohr had most success, battling on to finish second overall behind the Alfa Romeo GTAm of eventual championship winner Toine Hezemans. The other two Capris – driven by Glemser and Yvette Fontaine – suffered engine problems and retired. The picture became even worse at the next round in Austria: not a single Capri finished, through reliability problems or racing incidents. Thereafter, nothing seemed to go right. Glemser came second at Budapest and fifth at Brno and Silverstone, but these were the only glimmers of light.

The worst disaster occurred, embarrassingly for the

Cologne team, at the Nürburgring. Three Capris were entered, and three Capris retired with engine problems. As a consequence Ford did not even attend the following ETC round, the 24-hour event at Spa-Francorchamps. Jochen Mass, who had some success in the European Hillclimb Championship that year in Capris, was signed to drive in the ETC championship for the penultimate race at Zandvoort but in fact only put in practice laps. The last event at Jarama also saw a complete Capri fiasco.

The only light at the end of the tunnel was the arrival of the RS2600. First shown as early as March 1970 at Geneva, it took a while for it to be homologated and even longer for it to enter production, but it was ready for the 1971 season.

The preparations had not been without a lot of hard effort. Together with Martin Braungart, who had been responsible for the chassis work on the 1970 cars,

At the first race of the 1973 ETC season, Jackie Stewart and Dieter Glemser took pole position. This busy pit lane scene betrays the fact that camshaft problems would end their race early.

Englishman Peter Ashcroft was drafted in to work miracles on the engine front. The basic V6 engine of 2637cc was derived from the Taunus 26M, but expanded for racing use in 1971 initially to 2873cc and then, from mid-season, to 2933cc. It was also given a lightened flywheel, a new Weslake crank, tougher bearings, enlarged valves, tweaked injection and dry-sump lubrication. Power shot up straight away to 275bhp, eventually reaching 285bhp with the later 2933cc units.

The suspension was much modified, with aluminium hubs, rear coil spring/damper units and aluminium torque arms/Watts linkage. The front discs became ventilated, and at the rear solid discs were fitted. The engine was also sited lower and more towards the rear to help handling.

Earning its nickname of 'Plastikbombe', it had flared glass-fibre wings, bonnet, doors and boot, plus a big front spoiler. The blue-and-white livery which would so distinguish Capris arrived mid-season, in August.

The opening event at Monza was a mixture of promise and frustration. Despite gaining pole and scoring a lap record, Glemser and Spaniard Alex Soler-Roig

retired with a blown gasket, and the François Mazet/Helmut Marko combination could do no better than tenth overall, beset by engine problems.

However, for the rest of the ETC season, the Capri was unstintingly reliable as well as extremely quick. A 1-2-3 in Austria was followed by outright wins at Brno, the Nürburgring, Spa-Francorchamps and Paul Ricard. Glemser was the undoubted star of the season, the winner of each of those events. He took the 1971 drivers' title, although class successes meant that Alfa Romeo beat Ford to the manufacturers' spoils.

After some successful hillclimbing in a Capri, Mass dominated the German Championship that year, failing to win only two of the eight rounds. Other highlights of the '71 season included Glemser's second place in the Jochen Rindt Memorial at Hockenheim, a class win for Glemser/Mass at the Kyalami Nine Hours in South Africa, and some success for Mass in the Springbok series in southern Africa (Ford won the saloon car title in this series).

In 1972, the Capri performed even better in the ETC Championship, despite the fact that both Neerpasch and Braungart had defected to BMW. Michael Kranefuss stepped into Neerpasch's shoes and basically continued the approach his predecessor had been taking.

Now boasting a stronger 290bhp 2933cc version of the RS2600 engine, the Capri was even quicker. The engine was given a higher (11.5:1) compression ratio and reprofiled cams. One big change was a step up to 15in diameter wheels from 13in, and wheel width expanded to 12in at the back, 10in up front.

Following his outright success in the 1971 German Championship in a Capri, Mass moved into the ETC team, partnered on occasion by Hans Stuck. The other

Jochen Mass and John Fitzpatrick (above) drove an excellent race at the 1973 Spa-Francorchamps 24 Hours to finish second. The reason why the Capri did not make much impact in 1973 can be seen behind the Jochen Mass car at Silverstone (right): the 'Batmobile' BMW CSL had homologated aerodynamic aids and the Capri did not. It was no contest.

regulars were Glemser and Soler-Roig. Many others made cameo appearances in the championship, including such famous names as Jackie Stewart, François Cevert and Ronnie Peterson.

The Capris stormed away with the '72 ETC season, winning all but one of the nine races, although, intriguingly, a British-based Capri driven by Brian Muir and John Miles actually beat the factory-backed Capris of Stewart/Cevert and Mass/Larrousse/Soler-Roig in the Paul Ricard Six Hours. Mass secured the drivers' championship, although Alfa Romeo again snatched the manufacturers' title thanks to their clean class score sheet.

Capris also won the Belgian and German national championships (with Claude Bourgoignie and a masterful Hans Stuck respectively), while Timo Makinen won the Finnish ice racing championship. At the 1972 Le Mans, Capris finished 10th and 11th, the Birrell/Bourgoignie partnership pulling off a class win into the bargain. And in the Nürburgring 1000km, Glemser/Mass came home seventh overall (and first in class) with Stuck/Soler-Roig following in eighth.

For the 1973 season, Alfa Romeo were out of the reckoning and the big – indeed, sole – competition came from BMW. Ford had a new trump card for this year, however, in the form of a number of star drivers: Jackie Stewart, Jody Scheckter and even Emerson Fittipaldi. However, the regular drivers remained Glemser and Mass, with John Fitzpatrick being the other frequent driver. Gerry Birrell was to have been another regular, but that plan was stopped short by his tragic death at Rouen in June 1973.

Mechanically, the engine was bored out by an extra millimetre to make 2995cc, and Weslake again worked its magic on reprofiling the camshaft and enlarging the valves. Combined with new under-bonnet ducting, the power output burst the 300bhp barrier, the official figure going as high as 325bhp. But this was still some way short of the BMW CSL's output of 350-370bhp.

New face Thomas Ammerschlager was responsible for the major new bodywork modifications that year. A deeper wrap-around front spoiler and squarer wings were specified after wind-tunnel testing, the rear wings incorporating ventilation slots to cool the tyres and improve air flow. And a new roll cage improved stiffness.

Suspension was again improved, with stiffer springs and different geometry to allow lighter steering, since wheel widths were now up to 12in at the front and 14in at the rear. Brakes were upgraded too, with aluminium calipers and bigger four-wheel ventilated ATE discs.

In the first race of the ETC season at Monza,

Stewart/Glemser took pole position but suffered a broken camshaft in the race, allowing the Lauda/Muir BMW CSL to take first blood in the title contest. Lauda's BMW won again at Spa-Francorchamps (a non-ETC event), beating off the Mass Capri. The pattern was reversed at the Salzburgring, when the Glemser/Fitzpatrick duo scored the first Capri win of the year. This was followed up with a Glemser/Mass victory in Sweden.

The remainder of the ETC championship, however, went BMW's way, the best Capri performances being second placings at the Spa-Francorchamps 24 Hours and at Silverstone. Even Fittipaldi and Stewart could do nothing at the Nürburgring Six Hours.

Apart from Hans Heyer's sterling work in the German championship, the Capri always played second fiddle to the BMWs that year. All three Capris entered for the '73 Le Mans 24 Hours failed to finish (this would be Birrell's final drive in a Capri), while at the three non-ETC Nürburgring events that year (1000km, 24 Hours and 500km), Capris were soundly beaten. The only consolation came from wins in the Far East at Fuji (Hezemans/Mass/Glemser) and Macau (Moffat).

What gave the BMWs such a lead in the latter part of the season? Just one thing: the Batmobile! Ex-Ford man Martin Braungart was responsible for effecting the aerodynamic wings which made the BMW CSL invincible that year. In mid-season, it was noticed that FIA rules allowed for road-homologated wings to be used for racing. A double-quick development period saw the extensive CSL 'Batmobile' wings being fitted to road cars, and BMW had an instant aerodynamic advantage. This came too late for Ford to reply, for the '73 season at least.

In truth, the Capris had been rather evil-handling things that season and their rate of success was perhaps better than might be expected given the overall picture. Mass described their handling as "very difficult", Fittipaldi was scared he might roll his, while Fitzpatrick commented that it was "the worst handling racing car I have ever driven".

One final irony of the season was that BMW driver Toine Hezemans – who won the '73 ETC title for BMW – defected to Ford in time to race Capris in the final ebb of the season! Another coup was that Niki Lauda was hired by Ford for the coming year, but his path in fact led instead to the Ferrari Formula 1 team in 1974 and to two World Championship victories.

Meanwhile, in Britain Ford had decided to enter the 1973 Tour of Britain rally with 3.0-litre Capris. It entered three cars, driven by Roger Clark, Prince Michael of Kent and Dave Matthews, and Ford supported other

Three 3000GXL Capris were entered in the 1973 Tour of Britain, this one being Roger Clark's. Distributor problems knocked him back to 24th place, and the best Capri was privateer Gordon Spice, coming home second overall behind James Hunt's Chevrolet Camaro. The final British factory effort for Capris in Group 1 racing came in 1974 (above right) when Tom Walkinshaw drove this car to a class victory.

entrants. Ironically the best Capri result was privateer Gordon Spice, who came second overall behind James Hunt's Chevrolet Camaro. The best official Ford placing was Dave Matthews in fifth place. Ford switched over to the Escort in future years.

The last Ford foray into Group 1 racing in the UK was in 1974, when none other than Tom Walkinshaw drove the ex-Prince Michael of Kent car to a class championship victory.

Back to the ETC story, and for 1974 Ford retired the RS2600 engine programme and switched to the 'Essex' 3.0-litre V6. Cosworth had been given the job of producing a reliable racing engine from this unit, and

work had begun as early as May 1972. This was the programme which led to the RS3100 road car, the homologation version of the Capri racer.

Cosworth's course was to engineer belt-driven double overhead camshafts on each bank of cylinders and four valves per cylinder, and to fit forged aluminium pistons, Lucas fuel injection and Lucas Rita transistorised ignition. For racing purposes, the 3.1-litre base engine of the RS3100 was bored out to 100mm for a total capacity of 3421cc. The engine was dry-sumped and the standard block made as strong as possible within the regulations. Cosworth managed to achieve around 415bhp.

Obviously, Ford needed the same sort of aerodynamic aids as BMW for the 1974 season, so a duck-tail spoiler was tested as early as the Fuji race at the end of 1973. Further testing with Hezemans produced the ideal shape and height, while side skirts and a deeper front spoiler improved the situation still further, making the Capri far easier to handle.

The Essex-engined Capri was heavier than the RS2600-based car, and its weight distribution was also

Ford's 1974 ETC entrants gained from BMW-style aerodynamics, notably the rear spoiler. The RS3100 was now the homologated basis for the race car.

Glemser leads Niki Lauda in one of the future Formula 1 World Champion's few appearances in a Capri. This is at the 1974 Salzburgring, an event which neither car finished. After suffering from axle trouble, Glemser and Toine Hezemans (below) recovered to take second place overall in the Nürburgring Six Hours.

biased more towards the front. To move weight rearwards, the radiators were repositioned just in front of the rear wheels, and the rear arches had to be reshaped to accommodate them.

Other changes included magnesium hub carriers, far stiffer springs, uprated tyres on 16in wheels with magnesium centres (up to 12¼in wide front and 15¾in rear), an electric brake fluid pump and a triple-plate clutch. Mid-way through 1974 came water-cooled brakes.

The major problem as the 1974 season approached was the OPEC oil crisis. Western economies were shaken and Ford's competition budget was cut by 25 per cent. It became obvious that Ford could not assault the '74 season as a fully-committed team. Indeed, both BMW and Ford missed the first ETC event at Monza.

Both teams, however, attended the next event at the Salzburgring. Ford fielded two cars, driven by

Hezemans/Glemser and Lauda/Mass, but both cars ended up with expired engines. The third round remained unfought, but the next round at the Nürburgring was a classic, and the last occasion on which Capris and BMW CSLs battled. The Mass Capri and one of the CSLs had an accident, leaving the Hezemans/Glemser Capri to pick up second place to a Zakspeed Escort.

Thereafter, a Capri won at Zandvoort (drivers were Mass, Glemser, Hezemans and Stommelen) and at the last ETC race at Jarama (drivers Ludwig, Hezemans and Heyer). But in this patchy year for the Capri, it was not enough to win the title: that went to Ford's Escort, the drivers' title being won by Hans Heyer. The only other significant Capri success in 1974 was Rolf Stommelen's convincing record in the German championship.

At the end of 1974, Ford announced that both AVO in Britain and the Cologne competitions department

Privateer Gordon Spice was dominant in British Group 1 racing. Here he leads two other Capris at Silverstone on his way to winning the 1977 title.

The Capri II was ripe for racing by 1975, and here (left) Tom Walkinshaw is leading at Spa in Belgium. Gordon Spice again (above), this time in a 3.0-litre Capri III at Oulton Park. He dominated most rounds to win the 1979 Group 1 title.

would be closing. That effectively marked the end of the Capri's international competition career, although the RS3100 did make a few appearances in the 1975 German championship with Jochen Mass and Klaus Ludwig driving. Its final appearance was at the October 1975 Kyalami 1000kms, where Mass/Ludwig failed to finish.

By that stage, the Capri II had made its first fleeting appearance at the 1974 Spa 24 Hours. One car was driven by Tom Walkinshaw and John Fitzpatrick, another by Claude Bourgoignie and Yvette Fontaine. Walkinshaw led the race on a number of occasions but reliability problems beset the car.

Thereafter Boreham left the job of wringing the best out of the Capri to the privateers. Many were extremely successful, none more so than Gordon Spice, who won six straight Group 1 British Saloon Car Championships from 1975 to 1980, and also won the 1978 Spa 24 Hours.

The Martin brothers would repeat that Spa triumph in 1979 in a 3000S.

The next chapter in the works race Capri story occurred in 1978, when Ford and Zakspeed combined forces to mount a challenge in the German Group 5 Championship. Zakspeed was already very well known and trusted through its championship-winning work with Escorts. Group 5 was the most radical of the modified classes: only the engine block had to come from a standard production car, and then not necessarily that of the model entered.

As such, the Zakspeed Capri had a completely new structure of aluminium tubing. This 'chassis' was created by Helmut Barth and Bruno Bunk of Zakspeed and weighed a mere 70kg. On to this went a vaguely recognisable Capri steel superstructure above the waistline. The rest of the main body was made of

In 1978, Ford released details about the Zakspeed Turbo racer which would compete in Group 5 events in Germany. This is the wind tunnel scale model. The basis for all Zakspeed Capris was an extremely lightweight aluminium space frame. These racers bore little resemblance to any road-going Capri.

aluminium, the same material also being used for the floorpan, while the removable body panels (front and rear wings, bonnet and front spoiler) were made of Kevlar composite. There was an immense rear spoiler fixed to the back, incorporating an adjustable blade angle.

The whole body was restyled during extensive wind tunnel testing, notably featuring a very low front end. Overall length was considerably increased, by more than 24in, while the car was 78in wide and 45in high. Weight went down to a remarkably low 780kg, thanks in part to bonded-in Perspex side and rear windows.

The rest of the structure harked back to the 1974 Capri racers: MacPherson strut front suspension, Bilstein dampers, live rear axle and Watts linkage, aluminium diff, ZF five-speed gearbox, side-mounted radiators and so on. Bigger changes were evident in other areas. The brakes were water-cooled, cross-drilled, ventilated discs of Porsche origin, initially with double calipers but later with four-piston single calipers. Rear wheel diameter went up to 19in, although all four wheels were narrower at 10½in front and 13in rear.

For the engine, Zakspeed's considerable experience with turbocharging led them down this route. To qualify for the under 2.0-litre class, the turbocharged engine had to be tiny according to the normal 1.4:1 'equivalence factor' – 1427cc to be precise. Zakspeed based its engine on the Cosworth BDA, with an alloy double overhead camshaft head and four valves per cylinder. A KKK turbocharger and Garrett intercoolers were installed.

The engine closely resembled the Escort units used by Zakspeed earlier in the 1970s. In the Capri, it developed between 380bhp and 460bhp (depending on boost) at 9000rpm, a phenomenal output from such a compact engine with humble 'Kent' origins.

The Zakspeed Capri's first appearance was at a Formula 1 Grand Prix warm-up race at Hockenheim in July 1978, with Hans Heyer at the wheel. This was merely a preliminary outing, prior to more events being contested in the 1979 season. Austrian citizen and 1978 German champion Harald Ertl got his first season at the wheel of a Capri but Heyer had more ultimate success, winning his division that year. But it was not until 1980 that the Ford/Zakspeed team took the challenge all the way. Ertl drove one 1.4-litre car and Klaus Niedzwiedz piloted another, their cars now developing 500bhp.

For 1980, Zakspeed also decided they wanted to compete in the over 2.0-litre class as well as the smaller category. The engine size grew to 1746cc; multiplied by 1.4 for the turbo installation, that equalled 2443cc on paper. Kügelfischer mechanical fuel injection was a familiar sight, while the KKK turbocharger was one size bigger and came with twin intercoolers. Now power was up to an amazing 560bhp. Other mechanical changes involved a switch from aluminium hub carriers to magnesium, and from ZF to Getrag transmission.

Driven by Klaus Ludwig, this super-powerful Capri had a very large rear spoiler to generate enormous downforce, but this was banned later in the summer and Ludwig had his points stripped for a number of races; thus the spoiler had to be replaced with a smaller, detachable item. To compensate for the loss of downforce, the bodywork was revised to take advantage of the latest ground-effect devices, namely side skirts and a central tunnel underneath the car.

Despite the difficulties, Ludwig beat off the Porsches to win his division in the 1980 season. He would go one better in 1981, too, although at the wheel of a 1.4-litre Capri, taking the overall title that year. The larger class was contested by Manfred Winkelhock who, with up to 600bhp to play with, came home third overall in the championship. In 1982, Ford's attention moved away from

The ferocious Zakspeed 1.4-litre BDA based engine used double overhead camshafts and KKK turbocharging to extract a phenomenal 460bhp. And that rose as high as 500bhp by 1980. The Zakspeed Capri's first outing (below) was at Hockenheim in July 1978, driven by Hans Heyer. He would prove a convincing competitor in the German National Production Car championship.

Zakspeed made a major assault on the German championship in 1979. Despite not competing in all rounds, Hans Heyer won his division; he is seen (above) at Zandvoort. In 1980 (below), Ford also competed in the larger 1.7-litre class. Klaus Ludwig's ground-effect car, seen at the Nürburgring, won its division in 1980 and took the overall title in 1981.

the ageing Capri, and so Zakspeed was left to campaign the Capri only sporadically with Klaus Niedzwiedz driving. This was the swansong of these mighty Capris.

The final twist to the Capri works racer story is that ex-competitions manager Michael Kranefuss was posted to the US. Together with Zakspeed, in 1981 he instigated the transformation of the Group 5 Zakspeed Capri into a Mustang IMSA racer! The chassis and mechanical specifications were all but identical to the Capri, only the bodywork being slightly longer and wider. Its only win came at Brainerd Raceway, with Ludwig driving.

Yet that is not truly the end of the story. The basic Zakspeed Capri engine, which was producing such phenomenal power outputs by the end, made a competitive Formula 1 power plant in the 1985 Grand Prix season, with Jonathan Palmer driving.

Modified road Capris continued their crusade in the hands of private drivers well beyond the point where they might have been considered uncompetitive. Perhaps the highlight of the Capri 2.8i's success in the 1980s was second, third and fourth placings in the Snetterton 24 Hours in 1986. A 2.8i also finished in the 1986 Lombard RAC Rally, although well down in 32nd place. And the Capri continued to be campaigned long after production was axed by Ford.

Capris were truly international competitors. As well as their well documented triumphs in rallycross, European Touring Car championships, national championships in Britain and Germany and long-distance relay events, Capris were successfully campaigned in Australia, New Zealand, South Africa and America. Their legacy is a surprisingly consistent and impressive competition record stretching over two decades.

LEGACY OF THE CAPRI

The Capri name lived on as late as 1994 in the Australian-made Mazda-based drop-top.

Like most older cars, Capris have had to go through wilderness years of old banger status before acquiring a sustainable following of enthusiasts. That day has well and truly arrived, as drivers realise the many advantages of running a Capri as a classic. Its effective mix of traits has never been truly replaced.

A whole generation grew up thinking of Capris as loutish. Bodie and Doyle were tough and blokey in one, and Terry minded Arthur's business in one. The Capri became a low rent teenagers' posing device – surely the very definition of naffness – and it has taken many years and many thousands of cars through the crusher for the Capri to shake off its lowly image.

Today there is a serious club following for the Capri and owners regard it with the same passion as other more readily acknowledged classics. The Capri does have the advantage of a genuinely iconic position in the national psyche.

People were constantly writing off the Capri in the early 1980s, saying it had reached the end of the road, that

Ford would not bother continuing with it because production volumes were so small. One writer stated in May 1984 that 'it is no secret that the Capri is to be given the corporate chop later this year'. Yet it did continue, despite the fact that a 'replacement' had arrived in 1983.

That car was the Sierra XR4i, the quick three-door member of Ford's controversial new fleet car family. Many pundits saw it as the death knell for the Capri: after all, it too was a nimble rear-wheel drive hatchback and in addition it had all the kudos of a brand new design. But in reality it was not a spiritual successor to the Capri, as events proved. It was more of a 'refined, sophisticated touring car' as John Miles of *Autocar* put it, whereas the Capri was a 'niftily small, practical, simple, well-ventilated, easy to manage (in some ways crude) value-for-money package'. He had a point – the Capri 2.8i offered 130mph for just over £8000, while the heavier Sierra

Worst potential area of rust on any Capri is at the top rear of the front wings. Rust can extend down to the floorpan in bad cases, and up the windscreen pillar.

Another vital area to check is all around the suspension turret mounts. Corroded areas can be repaired but avoid cars with bodged previous repairs.

Perhaps the area of greatest concern for Capri restorers is the trim. It is not particularly durable and finding replacement parts can be very difficult, even for later cars like this black-and-gold Capri II S.

XR4i was no quicker and was £1000 more expensive.

The truth is that there has not been a spiritual descendant of the Capri from Ford. The next true coupé from Ford was an American one – the Probe. Arriving in January 1988, it was based on the Mazda 626 and was built by Mazda in Flat Rock, USA. As a front-wheel drive coupé, it could never have the same appeal as the Capri. Although it was marketed in continental Europe, it never came to the UK, unlike the second-generation Probe of 1992. Some journalists were tempted to hail it as the return of the Capri but it never fitted the bill.

The Capri name itself did not die with the European 'car you always promised yourself'. In America, it was used as the badge for the Mercury version of the '79 model year Ford Mustang III, and it too lasted until 1986. Then the name migrated to Australia, where Ford's locally produced sports convertible was so badged. Again this was something far removed from the European Capri, although it carried the right sporty connotations since the European Capri had been marketed in Australia.

The Australian Capri was designed by Ghia and based on the front-wheel drive Mazda 323 floorpan. It was a 2+2 with a choice of 1.6-litre twin cam (105bhp) and 1.6 turbo (136bhp) engines. Although it was made in sizeable numbers from 1988 until 1994, and was marketed in the US as the Mercury Capri, it never came to Europe as a listed model.

No, in Europe at least, the Capri name will always be linked with the classic rear-wheel drive Ford. The term 'classic' certainly applies to the Capri now. Whereas the RS2600 and RS3100 have always been regarded as collectable, it has taken mainstream Capris a little longer to gain a following. The Mk1 Capri naturally has the most respect in classic circles, particularly the big 3.0-litre V6, but other models are gaining fast.

Particularly sought-after cars include the Mk1 1600GT, Capri II 2000S and Ghia, all versions of the 3000, the 2.8i and its limited edition sister the 280, and, of course, the RS2600 and RS3100. Any one of the official and semi-official turbo cars is also worth keeping an eye out for.

The Capri has many attributes in ownership terms. Firstly it is a Ford, with all that that brings: reliability, simple servicing, ready tunability, generally cheap and plentiful parts, and plenty of specialist back-up. There are now several independent companies in the UK and Germany dedicated to the supply of Capri parts and the restoration of owners' cars.

Perhaps the most important aspect to consider when buying a Capri is originality and completeness. Particularly in early cars, the correct and unadulterated specification is preferred. Trying to assemble an authentic specification without a 100% complete car to start with can cause an awful lot of headaches. Most significantly, the complex system of decor groups can be confusing and awkward to duplicate – and the availability of original early trim parts is increasingly sparse.

Bodywork is very typical of any car of the Capri's age.

Rear-wheel drive, 150bhp and smart looks: it sounded like the death knell for the Capri, but in fact the Sierra XR4i was no substitute.

Rust will inevitably have some hold and, while it is generally fairly easy to repair, badly corroded specimens must be avoided. Broadly similar corrosion problems apply to all types of Capri.

Front wings have numerous mud traps where corrosion sets in first, but front wings are bolt-on and easy to replace when available. Areas to check include the space around the headlamps, the join between the front valance and wing (look behind the bumper), lower rear edges, wheelarches and where the inner wings butt up against the outer wings. Pay particular attention to the tops of the wings, especially at the back, as serious rust here can extend to the bulkhead, door pillars, windscreen pillars and even down to the floorpan.

Also check the front MacPherson suspension turrets for corrosion and signs of earlier repairs. The areas of metal around the three mounting holes can be repaired, but the work must be done correctly using proper repair panels and continuous welding. Avoid examples with filler, rivets or tack welds in this area. Rear wings suffer in the same sort of way. Problems usually start in the wheelarches and can extend back down to the rear corners and the leading edges where they meet the sills; but repair sections are readily available.

Sills do rust, especially on older cars; if the drain holes are blocked, you can be sure that trouble is lurking. Check the outer sills for signs of previous repair, then make sure the jacking points are sound. Also lift the carpets to check for rust in the inner sills, especially where they join the floorpan. It is worth looking all over the floorpan for tell-tale signs of rust, as well as under the dash, where door pillars and bulkhead should be checked.

Have a good look at the strengthening box sections underneath the car. A prod around will be needed to ensure that any trouble is not simply covered over with underseal. Problem areas include the cross-member on to which the front anti-roll bar bolts, the box sections behind the front wheels, and the box sections which kick up over the rear axle. You must also check the rear leaf spring hanger mountings.

Next to the opening panels. The doors themselves rust from the bottom upwards and have a tendency to lose integrity around the window frames. They can also drop if the hinge pins are worn. The leading inside edge of the bonnet is susceptible to rot, as well as the lower edges of the boot lid, or hatch on the Capri II and III. Another point to consider is the accumulation of moisture under vinyl roofs; look for tell-tale signs of blistering.

If the bodywork sounds nightmarish, do not be put off too much. Most of it is repairable and you should only really worry if the door pillars, windscreen pillars or suspension mounting points are corroded. Front wings and many body parts for Mk1 Capris are now unavailable, so repair – or the lucky discovery of second-hand panels – will often be your only solution.

On the mechanical side, the worries are much less severe. All the mainstream engines are simple, durable and extremely well supported from a parts and specialist point of view. None of the standard engines was highly tuned, all having come directly from other models.

The five-bearing 'Kent' engines (1300 and 1600) are extremely common and simple. Signs of piston wear include oil fumes from the filler cap and a smoky exhaust. However, oil in the water may not be the head gasket problem it seems: the cylinder block may have cracked and a replacement block will be needed. Otherwise, it is all straightforward; make the usual checks for timing chain rattle, noisy valve gear and low oil pressure.

Post-1972, the 1600 engine became the Pinto overhead camshaft unit; the 2000 engine in the Capri II is also from the same family. Neglect of these engines can cause camshaft and cam follower wear, which will mean a head-off repair (or major work if a follower fails when the engine is running). High mileage engines use a lot of oil and leaks around the camshaft cover are a common problem, as are leaky water pumps.

On Mk1 Capris, the 2000GT V4 engine derives from the Corsair and it would be fair to say that it has a poor reputation. The V4 is not a common sight these days and with good reason. Parts are hard to come by and reliability is far from perfect. The main problems are blown head gaskets, oil leaks, noisy valve gear and failing oil pumps. Original fibre timing gears are weak and should be replaced with steel ones.

The big 'Essex' V6 3000 engine remains very sought-after in Capris. It is reliable provided that it has not been over-revved, but problems include overheating, blown head gaskets, worn fibre timing gears, weak oil pump shafts, excessive oil consumption, bearing rumble, warped heads and worn valve gear. Parts are becoming more difficult to find.

Probably the best engine choice is the 'Cologne' 2.8-litre V6 with its durable and reliable Bosch fuel injection. Problems in the injection system will reveal themselves in high-speed misfires, which can be expensive to fix. Make the usual checks for tappet noise and exhaust smoke.

Similarly, there is no need to fret over gearboxes, usually four-speeders, although all post-1983 2000 and 2.8i models, and some 1600s, had five speeds. Bearings do wear and second gear synchromesh often grows weak, but repair/replacement is very simple; watch also for a 'box jumping out of gear. Listen for a worn propshaft and differential, and change quality on all 'boxes should be smooth. The five-speed 'box is certainly preferable in modern road conditions, but in the 2.8i it makes the car slower and the change is not as smooth as the 1981–82 four-speeder.

The automatic gearbox on Mk1 Capris was the Borg Warner Type 35 three-speed unit. For Capri II models the tough Ford C3 auto 'box was substituted, and both units are reliable. Automatic is rarely found on a four-cylinder car, but 3.0-litre V6 versions are very commonly fitted with self-shifters.

Rear axles are tough, but rear leaf springs can crack and sag after prolonged use. Noisy axles are not necessarily a sign of trouble. At the front, check for soft dampers. Loose steering and worn bushes in the suspension and anti-roll bar may reveal themselves by a wobble through the wheel, although warped front discs can have the same effect under braking. Power steering (on late model V6 cars only) can lose fluid.

Alloy wheels – of a number of different designs – are a desirable fitment but are prone to damage from kerbing. They can also become corroded, which looks unsightly but effective refurbishment is easy enough.

Perhaps the most vital point to consider when buying a Capri is its trim. This gives the particular model its distinct identity and everything needs to be present because finding replacements, even for late-model Capris, will be a real challenge.

Interiors do not last particularly well, the seats especially wearing quickly. Fitting replacement items may be easy, but the big headache is finding them in the first place. Capri Mk1 and II trim bits such as map reading lights, chrome strips and other brightwork are very rare, and even Capri III items are becoming scarce.

The RS models are a special case. Only 3532 RS2600s were made, and there were no official imports to Britain. A handful exist in the UK but most are still to be found in Germany. The RS3100 is a much rarer beast, a mere 248 having been made. Genuine survivors are extremely scarce, and it is not unknown for an amateur replica to be passed off as a real RS. Check the identity carefully and, if in doubt, consult one of the Capri clubs.

It is unusual to find a completely original RS these days. Even those that have been carefully returned to their original appearance and condition may well have substitute 3.0-litre engine blocks, incorrect suspension and missing trim. It is now virtually impossible to find items like wings and bumpers, while even simple RS components like the clutch and exhaust are unavailable.

Likewise, genuine Series X Capris are rare and many ordinary Capris have been converted more recently using inferior reproduction panels and parts. The original glass-fibre body panels are still made by Fibresports.

Coachbuilders Tickford are very much alive and well, and still in a position to support the Tickford Capri Turbo from a parts and restoration point of view. Only 100 genuine cars were made and all attract significant premiums on the market – examples can still change hands for the same sum that they cost new. Again there are many after-market Tickford-inspired goodies, in particular the effective A-frame rear end.

Overall, owning a Capri today is genuinely practical. Restoration is relatively simple, the mechanics are generally reliable, and cars can be very durable if they are looked after. Above all, Capris are *enjoyable* to own, a reminder of a time when things were done very differently from today, an age of rear-drive entertainment and a more carefree age of 'style'. Perhaps it is time to promise yourself the Capri all over again…

APPENDIX

UK and German production figures

		1300	1500	1600	1700	2000	2300	2600[1]	2800	3000	Kits	Total	Grand total UK/D
1968	UK[2]										15	3097	3855
	D[2]											758	
1969	UK[3]										13910	79635	213979
	D	26338	37100		51670	10432	8804					134344	
1970	UK	[4]		[4]		8777				11100	15800	84973	254713
	D	40062	29771	27282	42768	17651	9870	2336				169740	
1971	UK	5347		26721		5124				3921	6035	47148	215874
	D	21692	22047	6778	24520	81834	3109	8746				168726	
1972	UK[5]	4280			30135	4825				4050	250	47005	199125
	D	8609	4657	12944	5469	69190	3348	46998		905		152120	
1973	UK[6]										1100	49392	233325
	D	14669		34679		50480	4839	51387	25735	2144		183933	
1974	UK	2222		28880		6133				1042	655	38932	185361
	D	20827		33458		43910	6245		38374	3615		146429	
1975	UK[7]	3158		13271		2130				213	450	21225	100051
	D	5889		16932		1095	30529		23568	813		78826	
1976	UK	4030		15508		6432				1063		27033	101102
	D	5661		21337		14250	10476		18229	4116		74069	
1977[8]		5448		35858		24991	10076		9659	5555		91587	91587
1978		3070		25248		26412	9466			4916		69112	69112
1979		3246		36329		31345	6534			7966		85420	85420
1980		1348		19032		16228	3016			2131		41755	41755
1981		582		16162		9567	1669		5747	931		34658	34658
1982				12659		7650	1432		4091			25832	25832
1983				11483		8793	1575		5767			27618	27618
1984				7709		5818	1366		4615			19508	19508
1985				4373		3175			1714			9262	9262
1986				4608		3444			2658			10710	10710
TOTAL UK		44500[9]		240000[9]		84000[9]				30000[9]		**398440**	
TOTAL D		157441	93575	326907	124427	426265	112354	109467	140157	33092		**1524407**	
TOTAL UK/D		202000[9]	93575	567000[9]	124427	510000[9]	112354	109467	140157	63100[9]		**1922847**	**1922847**

Notes [1] 2600 figures should include 3532 RS2600 models, produced as follows: 1970, 53; 1971, 752; 1972, 1360; 1973, 1188; 1974, 178; 1975, 1. [2] No model split figures are available for 1968. [3] No model split figures are available for 1969 UK production, but 42073 GT models and 37562 standard models were made. [4] No distinction was made in the 1970 Halewood production log between 1300GT and 1600GT models. The available figures are as follows: 1300, 7838; 1600, 21525; 1300GT/1600GT, 19933. [5] Split figures are only available for Jan-Nov 1972, and are quoted in the columns; a further 3465 cars (model not known) were built at Halewood in December and these are included in the 1972 UK total. [6] No model split records remain for 1973 UK. These should also include 248 RS3100 Capris. [7] In 1975, UK 'Midnight' Capri S models were grouped together in the production logs without engine size being recorded (total: 2003, which is included in the 1975 UK total). [8] All UK production ceased in October 1976, so figures from 1977 on are Cologne only. [9] These model split totals are approximate.

A note about the production figures There is little doubt or controversy about the accuracy of German production figures, although inevitably there is a very slight discrepancy between the model split totals and the yearly totals. However, the Halewood figures quoted above differ significantly from previously published Capri production tallies, which were probably arrived at by subtracting Cologne production from Ford of Europe's quoted grand total Capri production. The information above has been compiled by the author from the original Halewood production logs, which must be regarded as the most reliable source. Knock-down kits for export were manufactured exclusively at Halewood. The total number of Capris built has been revised to 1,922,847.

Production by type: Capri Mk1: 1,209,100; Capri II: 404,169; Capri III: 309,578

Summary of Capri models.................

CAPRI Mk1 UK MARKET 1300 (1969-72), L (1969-73), X (1969-70), XL (1969-72); **1300GT** (1969-71), L (1969-71), X (1969-70), R (1969-70), XL (1969-71), XLR (1969-71); **1600** (1969-72), L (1969-73), X (1969-70), XL (1969-73); **1600GT** (1969-72), L (1969-72), X (1969-70), R (1969-70), XL (1969-72), XLR (1969-72); **2000GT** (1969-73), L (1969-72), X (1969-70), R (1969-70), XL (1969-72), XLR (1969-72); **3000GT** (1969-73), L (1969-72), X (1969-70), R (1969-70), XL (1969-72), XLR (1969-72), E (1970-72), GXL (1972-73); **RS3100** (1973) **Special Editions** Capri Special (Nov 1971) – based on 1600GT/2000GT; Capri S (May 1972) – based on 1600GT/ 2000GT/ 3000GT **GERMAN MARKET 1300** (1969-73); **1500** (1969-72); **1600XL** (1972-73), GT (1972-73); **1700GT** (1969-72), R (1969-70); **2000** (1969-72), R (1969-70); **2300GT** (1969-73), R (1969-70); **2600GT XLR** (1970-72), GT (1972-73); **RS2600** (1970-74); **3000GXL** (1972-73) **Note** X and L packs available as in the UK until Sep 1970. R was initially a separate model based on the GT models and 90bhp 2000. From Sep 1970 until Sep 1972, L, XL and XLR packs were offered, as in the UK.

CAPRI II UK MARKET 1300 (1975-78), L (1974-78); **1600L** (1974-78), XL (1974-75), GL (1975-78), GT (1974-75), S (1975-78); **2000GL** (1975-78), GT (1974-75), S (1975-78), Ghia (1974-78); **3000GT** (1974-75), S (1975-78), Ghia (1974-78) **Special Editions** Capri S [JPS/Midnight] (Mar-Jun 1975) – based on 1600GT/2000GT/3000GT, Series X packs available from Aug 1977 **GERMAN MARKET 1300L** (1974-78), XL (1974-76), GL (1976-78) **Note** 1300GT (1974-78) offered in Italy and France only; **1600L** (1974-78), XL (1974-76), GL (1976-78), GT (1974-76), Ghia (1974-76); **2000GL** (1976-78), S (1976-78), Ghia (1976-78); **2300GT** (1974-76), S (1976-78), Ghia (1974-78); **3000GT** (1974-76), S (1976-78), Ghia (1974-78)

CAPRI III UK MARKET 1300 (1978), L (1978-82); **1600L** (1978-82), LS (1981-84), GL (1978-82), S (1978-80), Laser (1984-86); **2000GL** (1978-82), S (1978-84), Ghia (1978-82), Laser (1984-86); **3000S** (1978-81), 3000 (1978-81), **2.8i** (Jun 1981-84), Injection Special (1984-86) **Special Editions** Capri GT4 (Feb 1980) – based on 1600, Capri Calypso (Aug 1981) – based on 1600, Capri Cameo (Aug 1981) – based on 1300/1600, Capri Tempo (Aug 1981) – based on 1300/1600, Capri Cabaret (Mar 1982) – based on 1600/2000, Capri Calypso II (May 1982) – based on 1600, Capri Cabaret II (Dec 1982) – based on 1600/2000, Capri Tickford 2.8 Turbo (Sep 1983 and on) – based on 2.8i, Capri Laser (Jun 1984) – based on 1600/2000, Capri 280 [Brooklands] (1987) – based on 2.8i **GERMAN MARKET 1600L** (1978-82), GL (1978-81), GT (1982-83); **2000L** (1978-81), GL (1978-81), S (1978-83), GT (1983-84), Super GT (1984); **2300S** (1978-84), Ghia (1978-82), Super GT (1984); **3000S** (1978-81), Ghia (1978-81); **2.8i** (1981-84), Turbo (1981-82), Super Injection (1984) **Special Editions** Capri GT4 (Nov 1979) – based on 1600

Specifications ....

CAPRI MK1 (UK MARKET)

1300 (1969-73) Engine Four-cylinder in-line **Crankshaft** Five main bearings **Bore × stroke** 80.98mm × 62.99mm (3.19in × 2.48in) **Capacity** 1298cc (79.2 cu in) **Valves** Overhead valves **Compression ratio** 9.0:1 **Fuel system** Single Motorcraft GPD carburettor **Maximum power** 52bhp at 5000rpm (57bhp at 5700rpm from 1970) **Maximum torque** 66lb ft (9.1kgm) at 2500rpm (66 lb ft (9.1kgm) at 3000rpm from 1970) **Transmission** Four-speed manual gearbox, fully synchronized **Gear ratios** 4th 1.00, 3rd 1.41, 2nd 2.40, 1st 3.54, rev 3.96 **Final drive** 4.125 **Top gear speed per 1000rpm** 16.3mph (26.2kmh) **Brakes** Front disc/rear drum, optional servo **Wheels/tyres** Steel disc wheels (4.5 × 13in), with 6 × 13in cross-ply tyres; optional Rostyle 5.5in wheels with 165/30 tyres (5in wheels standard from Sept 1972) **Length** 167.8in (4262mm) **Wheelbase** 100.8in (2559mm) **Width** 64.8in (1646mm) **Height** 50.7in (1288mm) **Front track** 53in (1346mm) **Rear track** 52in (1321mm) **Unladen weight** 1940lb (880kg) **Top speed** 84mph (86mph (138kmh) from 1970) **0-60mph** 23.0 secs (22.0 secs from 1970)

1300GT (1969-71) As 1300 except: **Compression ratio** 9.2:1 **Fuel system** Weber carb **Maximum power** 64bhp at 6000rpm (72bhp at 5500rpm from 1970) **Maximum torque** 64.5lb ft (8.9kgm) at 4000rpm (65lb ft (9.0kgm) at 2500rpm from 1970) **Tyres** 165/13 radial-ply **Height** 50.2in (1275mm) **Unladen weight** 1985lb (900kg) **Top speed** 93mph (150km), 94mph (151kmh) from 1970 **0-60mph** 14.8 secs

1600 (1969-72) As 1300 except: **Bore × stroke** 80.98mm × 77.62mm (3.19in × 3.05in) **Capacity** 1599cc (97.5cu in) **Compression ratio** 9.0:1 **Maximum power** 64bhp at 4800rpm (68bhp at 5700rpm from 1970) **Maximum torque** 85lb ft (11.75kgm) at 2500rpm **Transmission** Optional Borg Warner 35 three-speed automatic **Final drive** 3.900 (4.125 optional) **Top gear speed per 1000rpm** 17.3mph (27.7 kmh) **Brakes** Servo optional 1969-70, standard from 1970 on **Unladen weight** 1985lb (900kg) **Top speed** 90mph (92mph (148kmh) from 1970) **0-60mph** 15.5 secs (15.0 secs from 1970)

1600GT (1969-72) As 1600 except: **Compression ratio** 9.2:1 **Fuel system** Weber twin-choke carburettor **Maximum power** 82bhp at 5400rpm (86bhp at 5700rpm from 1970) **Maximum torque** 92lb ft (12.7kgm) at 3600rpm **Gear ratios** 4th 1.00, 3rd 1.40, 2nd 2.01, 1st 2.97, rev 3.32 **Final drive** 3.78 **Top gear speed per 1000rpm** 17.9mph (28.6kmh) **Brakes** Standard servo from launch **Tyres** 165/13 radial-ply **Height** 50.2in (1275mm) **Unladen weight** 2030lb (921kg) **Top speed** 96mph (155kmh), 100mph (160kmh) from 1970 **0-60mph** 14.6 secs (13.4 secs from 1970)

1600 (1972-73) As 1600 (1969-72) except: **Bore × stroke** 87.67mm × 66mm (3.45in × 2.60in) **Capacity** 1593cc (97.2 cu in) **Valves** Overhead camshaft **Compression ratio** 9.2:1 **Maximum power** 72bhp at 5500rpm **Maximum torque** 87lb ft (12kgm) at 2700rpm **Gear ratios** 4th 1.00, 3rd 1.41, 2nd 2.41, 1st 3.54, rev 3.96 **Final drive** 3.90 **Top gear speed per 1000rpm** 16.8mph (27.04kph) **Brakes** Standard servo **Wheels/tyres** 5 × 13in wheels with 165/13 radial-ply tyres **Unladen weight** 2121lb (962kg) **Top speed** 98mph (158kmh) **0-60mph** 13.0 secs

1600GT (1972-73) As 1600 (1972-73) except: **Fuel system** Weber 32/36 DGV carburettor **Maximum power** 88bhp at 5700rpm **Maximum torque** 92lb (12.7kgm) at 4000rpm **Final drive** 3.770 **Top gear speed per 1000rpm** 17.8mph (28.6kmh) **Unladen weight** 2024lb (920kg) **Top speed** 104mph (167kmh) **0-60mph** 11.5 secs

2000GT (1969-73) As 1300 except: **Engine** Four-cylinder vee formation at 60 degrees **Crankshaft** Three main bearings **Bore × stroke** 93.66mm × 72.44mm (3.69in × 2.85in) **Capacity** 1996cc (121.8 cu in) **Compression ratio** 8.9:1 **Fuel system** Weber carburettor **Maximum power** 92.5bhp at 5500rpm **Maximum torque** 104lb ft (14.38kgm) at 3600rpm **Transmission** Optional Borg Warner 35 three-speed automatic **Gear ratios** 4th 1.00, 3rd 1.40, 2nd 2.01, 1st 2.97, rev 3.32 **Final drive** 3.545 (3.440 from Oct 1970) **Top gear speed per 1000rpm** 19.0mph (30.4kmh), 19.4mph (31.2kmh) from Oct 1970 **Brakes** Standard servo **Tyres** 165/13 radial-ply **Height** 50.2in (1275mm) **Unladen weight** 2115lb (959kg) **Top speed** 106mph (171kmh) **0-60mph** 10.6 secs

3000GT/3000E (1970-71) As 1300 except: **Engine** Six-cylinder vee formation at 60 degrees **Crankshaft** Four main bearings **Bore × stroke** 93.66mm × 72.44mm (3.69in × 2.85in) **Capacity** 2994cc (182.7 cu in) **Compression ratio** 8.9:1 **Fuel system** Weber 40 DFAV twin-choke carburettor **Maximum power** 128bhp at 4750rpm **Maximum torque** 173lb ft (23.9kgm) at 3000rpm **Transmission** Optional Borg Warner 35 three-speed automatic **Gear ratios** 4th 1.00, 3rd 1.41, 2nd 2.21, 1st 3.16, rev 3.35 **Final drive** 3.220 **Top gear speed per 1000rpm** 20.7mph (33.3kmh) **Brakes** Standard servo **Wheels/tyres** 5 × 13in Rostyle wheels and 185/70 13 radial-ply tyres (175/13 for Australia) **Height** 50.2in (1275mm) **Unladen weight** 2330lb (1057kg) **Top speed** 114mph (183kmh) or 110mph (177kmh) automatic **0-60mph** 9.2 secs (11.4 secs automatic)

3000GT/3000E/3000GXL (1971-73) As 3000GT (1970-71) except: **Maximum power** 138bhp at 5300rpm (140bhp from Sept 1972) **Maximum torque** 174lb ft (24.1kgm) at 3000rpm **Gear ratios** 4th 1.00, 3rd 1.41, 2nd 1.94, 1st 3.16, rev 3.35 **Final drive** 3.090 **Top gear speed per 1000rpm** 21.9mph (35.2kmh) **Unladen weight** 2380lb (1079kg) **Top speed** 122mph (196kmh) or 118mph (190kmh) automatic **0-60mph** 8.3 secs (10.5 secs automatic)

RS3100 (1973-74) As 3000GT (1971-73) except: **Bore × stroke** 95.19mm × 72.44mm (3.75in × 2.85in) **Capacity** 3091cc (188.6cu in) **Fuel system** Weber 38 EGAS twin-choke carburettor **Compression ratio** 9.0:1 **Maximum power** 148bhp at 5000rpm **Maximum torque** 187lb ft (25.9kgm) at 3000rpm **Transmission** Manual only, optional limited slip differential **Top gear speed per 1000rpm** 22.6mph (36.4kmh) **Brakes** Ventilated front discs **Wheels** RS2600 cast alloy wheels with 6in wide rims **Length** 164.8in (1263mm) **Front track** 54.2in (1377mm) **Rear track** 53.2in (1351mm) **Unladen weight** 2315lb (1050kg) **Top speed** 125mph (201kmh) **0-60mph** 7.3 secs

Capri Mk1 (German market)

1300 (1969-72) Engine Four-cylinder vee formation at 60 degrees **Crankshaft** Three main bearings **Bore × stroke** 84mm × 58.9mm (3.31in × 2.32in) **Capacity** 1305cc (79.6 cu in) **Valves** Overhead valves **Compression ratio** 8.2:1 **Fuel system** Single Ford 28 carburettor **Maximum power** 50bhp at 5000rpm **Maximum torque** 69lb ft (9.5kgm) at 2500rpm **Transmission** Four-speed manual gearbox, fully synchronized **Gear ratios** 4th 1.00, 3rd 1.368, 2nd 1.968, 1st 3.424 (from Sept 1970: 4th 1.00, 3rd 1.37, 2nd 1.97, 1st 1.365, rev 3.66) **Final drive** 4.110 **Top gear speed per 1000rpm** 16.5mph (26.5kmh) **Brakes** Front disc/rear drum, optional servo **Wheels/tyres** Steel disc wheels (4.5 × 13in), with 6 × 13in tyres (optionally 165/13 tyres) **Length** 167.8in (4262mm) **Wheelbase** 100.8in (2559mm) **Width** 64.8in (1646mm) **Height** 52.3in (1330mm) **Front track** 53in (1346mm) **Rear track** 52in (1321mm) **Unladen weight** 2150lb (975kg) **Top speed** 83mph (133kmh) **0-100kmh** 24.0 secs

1300 (1972-73) As 1300 (1969-72) except: **Engine** Four-cylinder in-line **Crankshaft** Five main bearings **Bore × stroke** 79mm × 66mm (3.11in × 2.60in) **Capacity** 1293cc (78.9 cu in) **Valves** Overhead camshaft **Compression ratio** 8.0:1 **Fuel system** Single Ford carburettor **Maximum power** 55bhp at 5500rpm **Maximum torque** 67lb ft (9.3kgm) at 3000rpm **Gear ratios** 4th 1.00, 3rd 1.37, 2nd 1.97, 1st 1.365, rev 3.66 **Wheels** 5in rims **Top speed** 87mph (140kmh) **0-100kmh** 21.0 secs

1500 (1969-72) As 1300 (1969-72) except: **Bore × stroke** 90mm × 58.9mm (3.54in × 2.32in) **Capacity** 1498cc (91.4 cu in) **Compression ratio** 8.0:1 (9.0:1 from 1970) **Fuel system** Single Ford 28 carburettor (Ford 35 carburettor from 1970) **Maximum power** 60bhp at 5000rpm (65bhp at 5000rpm from Sept 1970) **Maximum torque** 83lb ft (11.5kgm) at 2400rpm (85lb ft (11.75kgm) at 2500rpm from Sep 1970) **Transmission** Optional Borg Warner 35 three-speed automatic **Final drive** 3.890 **Top gear speed per 1000rpm** 17.4mph (28kmh) **Top speed** 88mph (142kmh) or 89mph (144kmh) from 1970 **0-100kmh**

19.0 secs (18.0 secs from 1970), 2 secs slower with automatic

1600 (1972-73) As 1300 (1969-72) except: **Engine** Four-cylinder in-line **Crankshaft** Five main bearings **Bore × stroke** 87.67mm × 66mm (3.45in × 2.60in) **Capacity** 1593cc (97.2 cu in) **Valves** Overhead camshaft **Compression ratio** 9.0:1 **Maximum power** 72bhp at 5500rpm **Maximum torque** 87lb ft (12kgm) at 2700rpm **Transmission** Optional Borg Warner 35 three-speed automatic **Gear ratios** 4th 1.00, 3rd 1.37, 2nd, 1.97, 1st 3.65, rev 3.66 **Final drive** 3.750 **Top gear speed per 1000rpm** 17.9mph (28.8kmh) **Brakes** Standard servo **Wheels/tyres** 5x13 wheels with 165/13 tyres **Top speed** 96mph (155kmh) **0-100kmh** 16.0 secs (20.0 secs automatic)

1600GT (1972-73) As 1600 (1972-73) except: **Fuel system** Weber 32/36 DAGV carburettor **Maximum power** 88bhp at 5700rpm **Maximum torque** 92lb ft (12.7kgm) at 4000rpm **Unladen weight** 2194lb (995kg) **Top speed** 106mph (170kmh) **0-100kmh** 13.0 secs (16.0 secs automatic)

1700GT (1969-72) As 1300 (1969-72) except: **Bore × stroke** 90mm × 66.8mm (3.54in × 2.63in) **Capacity** 1699cc (103.7 cu in) **Compression ratio** 9.0:1 **Fuel system** Solex 32 carburettor **Maximum power** 75bhp at 5000rpm **Maximum torque** 95lb ft (13.1kgm) at 2500rpm **Transmission** Optional Borg Warner 35 three-speed automatic **Final drive** 3.700 **Top gear speed per 1000rpm** 18.5mph (29.8kmh) **Brakes** Standard servo **Unladen weight** 2160lb (980kg) **Tyres** Standard 165/13 **Top speed** 95mph (152kmh) **0-100kmh** 15.0 secs (17.0 secs automatic)

2000GT (1969-73) As 1300 (1969-72) except: **Engine** Six-cylinder vee formation at 60 degrees **Crankshaft** Four main bearings **Bore × stroke** 84mm × 60.14mm (3.31in × 2.37in) **Capacity** 1998cc (121.9 cu in) **Compression ratio** 8.0:1 (9.0:1 on optional R spec engine, standard from 1970) **Fuel system** Solex twin-choke 32/32 EEIT carburettor **Maximum power** 85bhp at 5000rpm (90bhp at 5000rpm on R spec engine, standard from 1970) **Maximum torque** 110lb ft (15.2kgm) at 3000rpm (113lb ft (15.6kgm) on R spec engine, standard from 1970) **Transmission** Optional Borg Warner 35 three-speed automatic **Final drive** 3.440 **Top gear speed per 1000rpm** 19.4mph (31.2kmh) **Brakes** Standard servo **Unladen weight** 2270lb (1030kg) **Wheels/tyres** Optional 5 × 13 wheels, standard 165/13 tyres **Top speed** 101mph (162kmh), or 103mph (165kmh) with 90bhp engine **0-100kmh** 13.0 secs, or 12.0 secs with 90bhp engine (2 secs slower with automatic)

2300GT (1969-73) As 1300 (1969-72) except: **Engine** Six-cylinder vee formation at 60 degrees **Crankshaft** Four main bearings **Bore × stroke** 90mm × 60.14mm (3.54in × 2.37in) **Capacity** 2293cc (139.9 cu in) **Compression ratio** 9.0:1 **Fuel system** Solex twin-choke 35 carburettor **Maximum power** 108bhp at 5000rpm (also available with 125bhp at 5500rpm 1969-70) **Maximum torque** 135lb ft (18.7kgm) at 3000rpm (or 136lb ft (18.8kgm) with 125bhp engine) **Transmission** Optional Borg Warner 35 three-speed automatic (108bhp engine only) **Final drive** 3.220 **Top gear speed per 1000rpm** 19.9mph (32.0kmh) **Brakes** Standard servo **Front track** 108bhp: as 1300; 125bhp: 53.2in (1352mm) **Rear track** 108bhp: as 1300; 125bhp: 52.2in (1327mm) **Unladen weight** 2293lb (1040kg) **Wheels/tyres** 4.5 × 13 wheels with 165/13 tyres; 125bhp: 5 × 13 wheels with 185/70 13 tyres **Top speed** 112mph (180kmh), or 115mph (185kmh) with 125bhp engine **0-100kmh** 11.0 secs with 108bhp engine (1 sec slower with automatic), or 10.0 secs with 125bhp engine

2600GT (1970-73) As 1300 (1969-72) except: **Engine** Six-cylinder vee formation at 60 degrees **Crankshaft** Four main bearings **Bore × stroke** 90mm × 66.8mm (3.54in × 2.63in) **Capacity** 2550cc (155.5 cu in) **Compression ratio** 9.0:1 **Fuel system** Solex twin-choke 35 carburettor **Maximum power** 125bhp at 5300rpm **Maximum torque** 150lb ft (20.75kgm) at 3000rpm **Transmission** Optional Borg Warner 35 three-speed automatic **Gear ratios** 4th 1.00, 3rd 1.37, 2nd 1.97, 1st 3.65, rev 3.66 **Final drive** 3.220 (3.090 from 1972) **Top gear speed per 1000rpm** 19.9mph (32.0kmh) **Brakes** Standard servo **Front track** 108bhp: as 1300; 125bhp: 53.2in (1352mm) **Rear track** 108bhp: as 1300; 125bhp: 52.2in (1327mm) **Unladen weight** 2293lb (1040kg) **Wheels/tyres** 5 × 13 wheels with 185/70 13 tyres **Top speed** 118mph (190kmh) **0-100kmh** 10.0 secs (11.0 secs automatic)

RS2600 (1970–74) As 1300 (1969-72) except: **Engine** Six-cylinder vee formation at 60 degrees **Crankshaft** Four main bearings **Bore × stroke** 90mm × 69mm (3.54in × 2.72in) **Capacity** 2637cc (160.9 cu in) **Compression ratio** 10.0:1 **Fuel system** Kügelfischer indirect mechanical fuel injection **Maximum power** 150bhp at 5800rpm (150bhp at 5600rpm from 1972) **Maximum torque** 166lb ft (23.0kgm) at 3500rpm (159lb ft (21.95kgm) from 1972) **Gear ratios** 4th 1.00, 3rd 1.37, 2nd 1.97, 1st 3.65, rev 3.66 (from 1972/73: 4th 1.00, 3rd 1.41, 2nd 1.94, 1st 3.16, rev 3.346) **Final drive** 3.220 (3.090 from 1972/73) **Top gear speed per 1000rpm** 19.9mph (32.0kmh), or 22.6mph (36.3kmh) with 3.090:1 axle **Brakes** Standard servo, Girling ventilated front discs from 1971 **Length** 164.8in (4186mm), 166.9in (4240mm) from 1972 **Height** 49.7in (1263mm), 50.5in (1283mm) from 1972 **Front track** 54.2in (1377mm), 54.8in (1392mm) from 1972 **Rear track** 53.2in (1352mm) **Unladen weight** 2315lb (1050kg), 2381lb (1080kg) from 1972 **Wheels/tyres** 6 × 13 alloy wheels with 185/70 13 tyres **Top speed** 126mph (202kmh) **0-100kmh** 8.6 secs

3000GT/GXL (1972–73)

As 3000GT/E/GXL (1971-73) under Capri Mk1 (UK market)

Capri Mk1 (American market)

1600 (1970–72) **Engine** Four-cylinder in-line **Crankshaft** Five main bearings **Bore × stroke** 80.98mm × 77.62mm (3.19in × 3.05in) **Capacity** 1599cc (97.5cu in) **Valves** Overhead valves **Compression ratio** 8.0:1 (8.4:1 in 1971) **Fuel system** Single Motorcraft carburettor **Maximum power** 71bhp SAE at 5000rpm (75bhp SAE at 5000rpm in 1971; 54bhp DIN at 4600rpm in 1972) **Maximum torque** 91lb ft (12.6kgm) SAE at 2800rpm (96lb ft (13.3kgm) SAE at 3000rpm in 1971; 80lb ft DIN at 2400rpm in 1972) **Transmission** Four-speed manual gearbox, fully synchronized **Gear ratios** 4th 1.00, 3rd 1.37, 2nd 1.97, 1st 3.65, rev 3.66 **Final drive** 3.890 **Top gear speed per 1000rpm** 17.4mph (28kmh) **Brakes** Front disc/rear drum **Wheels/tyres** Steel disc wheels (5 × 13in), with 165/13 tyres **Length** 167.8in (4262mm) **Wheelbase** 100.8in (2559mm) **Width** 64.8in (1646mm) **Height** 52.3in (1330mm) **Front track** 53in (1346mm) **Rear track** 52in (1321mm) **Unladen weight** 2135lb (968kg) **Top speed** 90mph (145kmh) **0-60mph** 17.3 secs (17.0 secs from 1971)

2000 (1971–74) As 1600 except: **Bore × stroke** 90.8mm × 76.9mm (3.57in × 3.03in) **Capacity** 1993cc (121.6 cu in) **Valves** Overhead camshaft **Compression ratio** 8.6:1 (8.2:1 from 1972) **Fuel system** Twin-choke carburettor **Maximum power** 100bhp SAE at 5600rpm (86bhp DIN at 5400rpm in 1972; 85bhp DIN at 5600rpm in 1973; 80bhp DIN at 5400rpm in 1974) **Maximum torque** 120lb ft (16.6kgm) SAE at 3600rpm (98lb ft (13.5kgm) DIN at 3000rpm in 1974) **Transmission** Optional three-speed automatic **Final drive** 3.440 **Top gear speed per 1000rpm** 19.4mph (31.2kmh) **Length** 173.8in (4415mm) from 1973 **Unladen weight** 2210lb (1002kg) **Top speed** 108mph (174kmh); 100mph (161kmh) from 1972 **0-60mph** 11.5 secs (13.5 secs from 1972)

2600 (1972–73) As 1600 except: **Engine** Six-cylinder vee formation at 60 degrees **Crankshaft** Four main bearings **Bore × stroke** 90mm × 66.8mm (3.54in × 2.63in) **Capacity** 2550cc (155.5 cu in) **Compression ratio** 8.2:1 **Fuel system** Holley-Weber twin-barrel carburettor **Maximum power** 107bhp at 5000rpm **Maximum torque** 130lb ft (18.0kgm) at 3400rpm **Transmission** Optional Borg Warner 35 three-speed automatic **Final drive** 3.220 **Top gear speed per 1000rpm** 19.9mph (32.0kmh) **Unladen weight** 2330lb (1057kg) **Tyres** 185/70 13 tyres **Top speed** 110mph (177kmh) **0-100kmh** 10.4 secs (12.0 secs automatic)

2800 (1974) As 1600 except: **Engine** Six-cylinder vee formation at 60 degrees **Crankshaft** Four main bearings **Bore × stroke** 93mm × 68.5mm (3.66in × 2.70in) **Capacity** 2792cc (170.8 cu in) **Compression ratio** 8.2:1 **Fuel system** Single twin-barrel carburettor **Maximum power** 105bhp at 4600rpm **Maximum torque** 140lb ft (19.4kgm) at 3200rpm **Transmission** Optional three-speed automatic **Final drive** 3.220 **Top gear speed per 1000rpm** 19.9mph (32.0kmh) **Unladen weight** 2341lb (1062kg) **Tyres** 185/70 13 tyres **Top speed** 105mph (169kmh) **0-100kmh** 10.0 secs (12.0 secs automatic)

Capri Mk1 (South Africa)

Perana V8 (1970–73) As 3000 (UK) except: **Engine** Eight-cylinder vee formation at 60 degrees **Crankshaft** Five main bearings **Bore × stroke** 101.6mm × 76.2mm (4.00in × 3.00in) **Capacity** 4949cc (302 cu in) **Compression ratio** 9.3:1 **Fuel system** Single four-barrel Holley 460 CFM carburettor **Maximum power** 281bhp at 5800rpm (SAE) **Maximum torque** 300lb ft (41.3kgm) at 3500rpm (SAE) **Transmission** Four-speed manual, optional three-speed Ford C4 automatic, Borg Warner limited slip diff **Gear ratios** 4th 1.00, 3rd 1.29, 2nd 1.69, 1st 2.32 **Final drive** 3.080 **Top gear speed per 1000rpm** 22.0mph (35.4kmh) **Unladen weight** 2352lb (1067kg) **Top speed** 143mph (231kmh) **0-60mph** 6.6 secs

Capri II (UK market)

1300 (1974–78) **Engine** Four-cylinder in-line **Crankshaft** Five main bearings **Bore × stroke** 80.98mm × 62.99mm (3.19in × 2.48in) **Capacity** 1298cc (79.2 cu in) **Valves** Overhead valves **Compression ratio** 9.2:1 **Fuel system** Single Motorcraft GPD carburettor **Maximum power** 57bhp at 5500rpm (50bhp at 5500rpm from Feb 1976 for base 1300) **Maximum torque** 67lb ft (9.3kgm) at 3000rpm (64lb ft (8.9kgm) at 3000rpm from Feb 1976) **Transmission** Four-speed manual gearbox, fully synchronized **Gear ratios** 4th 1.00, 3rd 1.40, 2nd 2.01, 1st 3.58, rev 3.32 **Final drive** 4.125 (optionally 4.444) **Top gear speed per 1000rpm** 16.3mph (26.2kmh) **Brakes** Front disc/rear drum, optional servo **Wheels/tyres** Steel disc wheels (5 × 13in), 165/13 tyres **Length** 168.8in (4288mm) **Wheelbase** 100.8in (2559mm) **Width** 66.9in (1698mm) **Height** 51.1in (1298mm) **Front track** 53.3in (1353mm) **Rear track** 54.5in (1384mm) **Unladen weight** 2227lb (1010kg) **Top speed** 89mph (143kmh), 85mph (137kmh) with 50bhp engine **0-60mph** 19.4 secs (20 secs with 50bhp engine)

1600 (1974–78) As 1300 except: **Bore × stroke** 87.67mm × 66mm (3.45in × 2.60in) **Capacity** 1593cc (97.2 cu in) **Valves** Overhead camshaft **Maximum power** 72bhp at 5500rpm **Maximum torque** 87lb ft (12kgm) at 2700rpm **Transmission** Optional Ford C3 three-speed automatic **Final drive** 3.770 **Top gear speed per 1000rpm** 17.8mph (28.6kmh) **Brakes** Standard servo **Unladen weight** 2293lb (1040kg) **Top speed** 98mph (157kmh) **0-60mph** 14.5 secs (16.0 secs automatic)

1600GT/1600S (1974–78) As 1600 except: **Fuel system** Weber 32/36 DGV twin-choke carburettor **Maximum power** 88bhp at 5700rpm **Maximum torque** 92lb ft (12.7kgm) at 4000rpm **Final drive** 3.750 **Top gear speed per 1000rpm** 18.0mph (28.9kmh) **Unladen weight** 2326lb (1055kg) **Wheels** 5.5in alloy wheels on S models **Top speed** 106mph (170kmh) **0-60mph** 13.5 secs (15.0 secs automatic)

2000GT/Ghia/S (1974–78) As 1300 except: **Bore × stroke** 90.8mm × 76.9mm (3.57in × 3.03in) **Capacity** 1993cc (121.6 cu in) **Valves** Overhead camshaft **Fuel system** Weber 32/36 DGV twin-choke carburettor **Maximum power** 98bhp at 5200rpm **Maximum torque** 112lb ft (15.5kgm) at 3500rpm **Transmission** Optional Ford C3 three-speed automatic **Gear ratios** 4th 1.00, 3rd 1.37, 2nd 1.97, 1st 3.65, rev 3.16 **Final drive** 3.440 **Top gear speed per 1000rpm** 19.5mph (31.4kmh) **Unladen weight** 2194lb (995kg) **Wheels** 5.5in alloy wheels on Ghia and S models **Top speed** 108mph (173kmh) **0-60mph** 11.1 secs

3000GT/Ghia/S (1974–78) As 1300 except: **Engine** Six-cylinder vee formation at 60 degrees **Crankshaft** Four main bearings **Bore × stroke** 93.66mm × 72.44mm (3.69in × 2.85in) **Capacity** 2994cc (182.7 cu in) **Compression ratio** 9.0:1 **Fuel system** Weber 40 DFAV twin-choke carburettor (later Weber 38/38 EGAS carburettor) **Maximum power** 138bhp at 5100rpm **Maximum torque** 174lb ft (24.1kgm) at 3000rpm **Transmission** Optional Ford C3 three-speed automatic (standard automatic on Ghia from 1976) **Gear ratios** 4th 1.00, 3rd 1.412, 2nd 1.94, 1st 3.16, rev 3.346 **Final drive** 3.090 **Top gear speed per 1000rpm** 21.9mph (35.2kmh) **Brakes** Standard servo **Wheels/tyres** 5.5in wide rims (later 6in) and 185/70 13 tyres **Unladen weight** 2580lb (1170kg) **Top speed** 122mph (196kmh) or 118mph (190kmh) automatic **0-60mph** 9.0 secs (10.5 secs automatic)

CAPRI II (GERMAN MARKET)

1300 (1974-78) Engine Four-cylinder in-line **Crankshaft** Five main bearings **Bore × stroke** 80.98mm × 62.99mm (3.19in × 2.48in) **Capacity** 1298cc (79.2 cu in) **Valves** Overhead valves **Compression ratio** 9.2:1 (8.0:1 from Aug 1974) **Fuel system** Single Ford carburettor **Maximum power** 55bhp at 5500rpm (54bhp at 5500rpm with 8.0:1 compression ratio; 73bhp for 1300GT – Italian and French market only) **Maximum torque** 67lb ft (9.3kgm) at 3000rpm (64lb ft (8.9kgm) at 3000rpm from Aug 1974) **Transmission** Four-speed manual gearbox, fully synchronized **Gear ratios** 4th 1.00, 3rd 1.40, 2nd 2.01, 1st 3.58, rev 3.32 **Final drive** 4.125 **Top gear speed per 1000rpm** 16.3mph (26.2kmh) **Brakes** Front disc/rear drum, optional servo **Wheels/tyres** Steel disc wheels (5 × 13in), 165/13 tyres **Length** 168.8in (4288mm) **Wheelbase** 100.8in (2559mm) **Width** 66.9in (1698mm) **Height** 51.1in (1298mm) **Front track** 53.3in (1353mm) **Rear track** 54.5in (1384mm) **Unladen weight** 2227lb (1010kg) **Top speed** 89mph (143kmh) **0-100kmh** 22.5 secs

1600 (1974-78) As 1300 except: **Bore × stroke** 87.67mm × 66mm (3.45in × 2.60in) **Capacity** 1593cc (97.2 cu in) **Valves** Overhead camshaft **Compression ratio** Also available as 8.2:1 **Maximum power** 72bhp at 5500rpm (68bhp at 5500rpm with low compression ratio, 63bhp for Swedish market) **Maximum torque** 85lb ft (11.8kgm) at 2800rpm (83lb ft (11.5kgm) with low compression ratio) **Transmission** Optional Ford C3 three-speed automatic **Final drive** 3.760 **Top gear speed per 1000rpm** 17.9mph (28.8kmh) **Brakes** Standard servo **Unladen weight** 2293lb (1040kg) **Top speed** 98mph (157kmh), or 93mph (150kmh) with low compression **0-100kmh** 17.0 secs (19.0 secs with low compression); 2 secs longer with automatic

1600GT/Ghia (1974-76) As 1600 except: **Fuel system** Weber 32/36 DAGV twin-choke carburettor **Maximum power** 88bhp at 5700rpm **Maximum torque** 92lb ft (12.7kgm) at 4000rpm **Final drive** 3.750 **Top gear speed per 1000rpm** 18.0mph (28.9kmh) **Unladen weight** 2326lb (1055kg) **Wheels/tyres** 5.5in alloy wheels on Ghia models, with 185/70 13 tyres on Ghia models **Top speed** 106mph (170kmh) **0-100kmh** 14.0 secs (16.5 secs automatic)

2000GL/S/Ghia (1976-78) As 1300 except: **Engine** Six-cylinder vee formation at 60 degrees **Crankshaft** Four main bearings **Bore × stroke** 84mm × 60.14mm (3.31in × 2.37in) **Capacity** 1998cc (121.9 cu in) **Compression ratio** 8.75:1 **Fuel system** Solex twin-choke 32/32 EEIT carburettor **Maximum power** 90bhp at 5000rpm **Maximum torque** 108lb ft (15.0kgm) at 3000rpm **Transmission** Optional Ford C3 three-speed automatic **Final drive** 3.440 **Top gear speed per 1000rpm** 19.4mph (31.2kmh) **Brakes** Standard servo **Unladen weight** 2469lb (1120kg) **Wheels/tyres** 5.5in alloys on S and Ghia models, with 185/70 13 tyres on S and Ghia models **Top speed** 106mph (170kmh) **0-100kmh** 14.0 secs, or 15.5 secs with automatic

2300GT/S/Ghia (1974-76) As 2000GL/S/Ghia except: **Bore × stroke** 90mm × 60.14mm (3.54in × 2.37in) **Capacity** 2293cc (139.9 cu in) **Fuel system** Solex twin-choke 35/35 EEIT carburettor **Maximum power** 108bhp at 5100rpm **Maximum torque** 128lb ft (17.7kgm) at 3000rpm **Final drive** 3.220 **Top gear speed per**

1000rpm 19.9mph (32.0kmh) **Top speed** 112mph (180kmh) **0-100kmh** 12.0 secs or 13.0 secs with automatic)

3000GT/S/Ghia (1974-78) As 2300 except: **Bore × stroke** 93.66mm × 72.44mm (3.69in × 2.85in) **Capacity** 2994cc (182.7 cu in) **Compression ratio** 9.0:1 **Maximum power** 138bhp at 5000rpm **Maximum torque** 170lb ft (23.5kgm) at 3000rpm **Transmission** Optional Ford C3 three-speed automatic (standard automatic on Ghia from 1976) **Gear ratios** 4th 1.00, 3rd 1.412, 2nd 1.94, 1st 3.16, rev 3.346 **Final drive** 3.090 **Top gear speed per 1000rpm** 21.9mph (35.2kmh) **Wheels/tyres** 5.5in wide alloy wheels and 185/70 13 tyres **Unladen weight** 2580lb (1170kg) **Top speed** 122mph (196kmh) or 118mph (190kmh) automatic **0-100kmh** 9.5 secs (10.5 secs automatic)

CAPRI II (AMERICAN MARKET)

2300 (1975-77) Engine Four-cylinder in-line **Crankshaft** Five main bearings **Bore × stroke** 96mm × 79.5mm (3.66in × 2.70in) **Capacity** 2300cc (140 cu in) **Valves** Overhead camshaft **Compression ratio** 9.0:1 **Fuel system** Single Holley-Weber twin-barrel carburettor **Maximum power** 88bhp at 5000rpm (91.5bhp from 1977) **Maximum torque** 116lb ft (16kgm) at 2600rpm (117lb ft (16.2kgm) at 2400rpm from 1977) **Transmission** Four-speed manual gearbox, fully synchronized (optional three-speed automatic) **Gear ratios** 4th 1.00, 3rd 1.37, 2nd 1.97, 1st 3.65, rev 3.66 **Final drive** 3.440 **Top gear speed per 1000rpm** 19.4mph (31.2kmh) **Brakes** Front disc/rear drum, servo assistance **Wheels/tyres** Steel disc wheels, optional alloys, 165/13 tyres **Length** 174.8in (4440mm) **Wheelbase** 100.8in (2559mm) **Width** 66.9in (1698mm) **Height** 51.1in (1298mm) **Front track** 53.3in (1353mm) **Rear track** 54.5in (1384mm) **Unladen weight** 2513lb (1140kg) **Top speed** 105mph (169kmh) **0-60mph** 13.0 secs

2800 (1975-77) As 2300 except: **Engine** Six-cylinder vee formation at 60 degrees **Crankshaft** Four main bearings **Bore × stroke** 93mm × 68.5mm (3.66in × 2.70in) **Capacity** 2792cc (170.8 cu in) **Compression ratio** 8.2:1 **Fuel system** Single Motorcraft 2150 twin-barrel carburettor **Maximum power** 109bhp at 4800rpm (110bhp from 1977) **Maximum torque** 146lb ft (20.2kgm) at 3000rpm (148lb ft (20.5kgm) at 2400rpm from 1977) **Final drive** 3.090 (or 3.220 in California) **Top gear speed per 1000rpm** 21.9mph (35.2kmh) or 19.9mph (32.0kmh) in California **Unladen weight** 2685lb (1218kg) **Tyres** 185/70 13 tyres **Top speed** 108mph (174kmh) **0-60mph** 10.5 secs (12.5 secs automatic)

CAPRI III (UK MARKET)

1300 (1978-82) Engine Four-cylinder in-line **Crankshaft** Five main bearings **Bore × stroke** 80.98mm × 62.99mm (3.19in × 2.48in) **Capacity** 1298cc (79.2 cu in) **Valves** Overhead valves **Compression ratio** 9.2:1 **Fuel system** Single Motorcraft GPD carburettor **Maximum power** 57bhp at 5500rpm (60bhp at 5750rpm from late 1979) **Maximum torque** 67lb ft (9.3kgm) at 3000rpm (68lb ft (9.4kgm) at 3000rpm from late 1979) **Transmission** Four-speed manual gearbox, fully synchronized **Gear ratios** 4th 1.00, 3rd 1.40, 2nd 2.01, 1st 3.58, rev 3.32 **Final drive** 3.890 or 4.125 **Top gear speed per 1000rpm** 17.3mph (27.9kmh) or 16.3mph (26.2kmh) with 4.125 axle ratio **Brakes** Front disc/rear drum, servo assisted **Wheels/tyres** Steel disc wheels (5 × 13in), 165/13 tyres (optional alloys with 185/70 13 tyres) **Length** 172.3in (4376mm) **Wheelbase** 100.9in (2563mm) **Width** 66.9in (1698mm) **Height** 52.1in (1323mm) **Front track** 53.3in (1353mm) **Rear track** 54.5in (1384mm) **Unladen weight** 2227lb (1010kg) **Top speed** 89mph (143kmh) or 91mph (146kmh) from 1979 **0-60mph** 20 secs (19.5 secs from 1979)

1600 (1978-86) As 1300 except: **Bore × stroke** 87.67mm × 66mm (3.45in × 2.60in) **Capacity** 1593cc (97.2 cu in) **Valves** Overhead camshaft **Maximum power** 72bhp at 5500rpm (73bhp at 5300rpm from late 1979) **Maximum torque** 87lb ft (12kgm) at 2700rpm (86lb ft (11.9kgm) from late 1979) **Transmission** Optional Ford C3 three-speed automatic, optional five-speed manual gearbox from 1983 (for gear ratios see 2000 model) **Final drive** 3.770 **Top gear speed per 1000rpm** 17.8mph (28.6kmh) **Unladen weight** 2293lb (1040kg) **Wheels/tyres** Sports wheels and 185/70 13 tyres on LS/Laser, 5.5in wheels on GL from 1980 **Top speed** 98mph (157kmh) **0-60mph** 13.5 secs

1600S (1978–80) As 1600 except: **Fuel system** Weber 32/36 DGV twin-choke carburettor **Maximum power** 88bhp at 5700rpm (91bhp at 5900rpm from late 1979) **Maximum torque** 92lb ft (12.7kgm) at 4000rpm **Final drive** 3.750 **Top gear speed per 1000rpm** 18.0mph (28.9kmh) **Unladen weight** 2326lb (1055kg) **Wheels/tyres** 5.5in or 6in alloy wheels and 185/70 13 tyres standard **Top speed** 106mph (170kmh) or 109mph from late 1979 **0–60mph** 12.5 secs (12.0 secs from late 1979), or 16.0 secs automatic (15.0 secs from late 1979)

2000 (1978–86) As 1300 except: **Bore × stroke** 90.8mm × 76.9mm (3.57in × 3.03in) **Capacity** 1993cc (121.6 cu in) **Valves** Overhead camshaft **Fuel system** Weber 32/36 DGV twin-choke carburettor **Maximum power** 98bhp at 5200rpm (101bhp from late 1979) **Maximum torque** 112lb ft (15.5kgm) at 3500rpm **Transmission** Four-speed manual gearbox (1978–83), five-speed manual gearbox (1983–86), optional Ford C3 three-speed automatic **Gear ratios** 1978-83: 4th 1.00, 3rd 1.37, 2nd 1.97, 1st 3.65, rev 3.16; 1983-86: 5th 0.825, 4th 1.00, 3rd 1.37, 2nd 1.97, 1st 3.65, rev 3.16 **Final drive** 3.440 **Top gear speed per 1000rpm** 21.4mph (34.4kmh) **Unladen weight** 2194lb (995kg) **Wheels/tyres** 5.5in or 6in wheels and 185/70 13 tyres standard **Top speed** 111mph (179kmh) **0–60mph** 10.8 secs

3000 (1978–81) As 1300 except: **Engine** Six-cylinder vee formation at 60 degrees **Crankshaft** Bore × stroke 93.66mm × 72.44mm (3.69in × 2.85in) **Capacity** 2994cc (182.7 cu in) **Compression ratio** 9.0:1 **Fuel system** Weber 38/38 EGAS carburettor **Maximum power** 138bhp at 5100rpm **Maximum torque** 174lb ft (24.1kgm) at 3000rpm **Transmission** Optional Ford C3 three-speed automatic **Gear ratios** 4th 1.00, 3rd 1.412, 2nd 1.94, 1st 3.16, rev 3.346 **Final drive** 3.090 **Top gear speed per 1000rpm** 21.9mph (35.2kmh) **Wheels/tyres** 6in alloy wheels with 185/70 13 tyres **Unladen weight** 2580lb (1170kg) **Top speed** 122mph (196kmh) or 118mph (190kmh) automatic **0–60mph** 8.5 secs (10.0 secs automatic)

3000 X-Pack (1978–80) As 3000 except: **Compression ratio** 9.1:1 **Fuel system** Triple Weber 42 DNCF twin-choke carburettors **Maximum power** 175bhp at 5000rpm **Maximum torque** 194lb ft (26.8kgm) at 4000rpm **Transmission** Limited slip differential standard **Brakes** Ventilated front discs **Wheels/tyres** 7.5 × 13in alloy wheels with 205/60 13 or 225/60 13 tyres **Width** 73in (1854mm) **Top speed** 130mph (209kmh) **0–60mph** 7.4 secs

2.8i (1981–86) As 1300 except: **Engine** Six-cylinder vee formation at 60 degrees **Crankshaft** Four main bearings **Bore × stroke** 93mm × 68.5mm (3.66in × 2.70in) **Capacity** 2792cc (170.4 cu in) **Compression ratio** 9.2:1 **Fuel system** Bosch K-Jetronic injection **Maximum power** 160bhp at 5700rpm **Maximum torque** 162lb ft (22.5kgm) at 4300rpm **Transmission** Four-speed manual (1981-84), five-speed manual (1984-86), limited slip diff standard from 1984 **Gear Ratios** 1981-84: 4th 1.00, 3rd 1.412, 2nd 1.94, 1st 3.16, rev 3.346; 1984-86: 5th 0.825, 4th 1.00, 3rd 1.26, 2nd 1.81, 1st 3.36, rev 3.37 **Final drive** 3.090 **Top gear speed per 1000rpm** 21.9mph (35.2kmh) with four speeds, 25.7mph (41.4kmh) with five speeds **Brakes** Ventilated front discs **Wheels/tyres** 7 × 13in alloy wheels with 205/60 13 tyres **Height** 51.1in (1298mm) **Unladen weight** 2712lb (1230kg) **Top speed** 130mph (210kmh) **0–60mph** 7.8 secs

Tickford Turbo Capri (1983–87) As 2.8i except: **Engine** Fitted with an IHI RHB6 turbocharger and Garrett AiResearch intercooler **Fuel system** Single point electronic fuel injection on boost **Maximum power** 205bhp at 5000rpm **Maximum torque** 260lb ft (36kgm) at 3000rpm **Transmission** Uprated five-speed gearbox, LSD **Brakes** Front and rear discs **Wheels/tyres** 7 × 15in wheels optional **Unladen weight** 2745lb (1245kg) **Top speed** 140mph (225kmh) **0–60mph** 6.0 secs

280 (1986) As 2.8i except: **Wheels/tyres** 7 × 15in alloy wheels with Pirelli P7 195/50 15 tyres

Capri III (German market)

1600 (1978–83) As 1600 (UK market) except: **Compression ratio** Also available as 8.2:1 (1978-80) **Maximum power** 72bhp at 5500rpm or 73bhp at 5300rpm from Nov 1979 (68bhp at 5500rpm or 70bhp at

5300rpm from Nov 1979 with low compression ratio) **Maximum torque** 85lb ft (11.8kgm) at 2800rpm or 86lb ft (11.9kgm) at 2700rpm from Nov 1979 (83lb ft (11.5kgm) with low compression ratio) **Transmission** Optional automatic not available on low compression model (1979-80 only) **Final drive** 3.980 with low compression engine (1979-80 only) **Unladen weight** 2293lb (1040kg) **Top speed** 98mph (157kmh), or 93mph (150kmh) with low compression **0–100kmh** 17.0 secs or 16.0 secs from Nov 1979 (19.0 secs or 16.5 secs with low compression); 2 secs longer with automatic

2000 (1978–81) As 1600 except: **Engine** Six-cylinder vee formation at 60 degrees **Crankshaft** Four main bearings **Bore × stroke** 84mm × 60.14mm (3.31in × 2.37in) **Capacity** 1998cc (121.9 cu in) **Compression ratio** 8.75:1 (8.2:1 from 1979) **Fuel system** Solex twin-choke 32/32 EEIT carburettor **Maximum power** 90bhp at 5000rpm **Maximum torque** 108lb ft (15.0kgm) at 3000rpm (104lb ft (14.4kgm) at 3000rpm from 1979) **Final drive** 3.440 **Top gear speed per 1000rpm** 19.4mph (31.2kmh) **Unladen weight** 2469lb (1120kg) **Wheels/tyres** 5.5in or 6in alloys on S and Ghia models, with 185/70 13 tyres on S and Ghia models **Top speed** 106mph (170kmh) **0–100kmh** 14.0 secs, or 15.5 secs with automatic

2000 (1979–84) As 2000 (UK) except: **Maximum power** 101bhp at 5200rpm **Unladen weight** 2337lb (1060kg) **0–100kmh** 13.0 secs (14.5 secs automatic)

2300 (1978–84) As 2000 (1978–81) except: **Bore × stroke** 90mm × 60.14mm (3.54in × 2.37in) **Capacity** 2293cc (139.9 cu in) **Fuel system** Solex twin-choke 35/35 EEIT carburettor **Maximum power** 108bhp at 5100rpm (114bhp at 5300rpm from Nov 1979) **Maximum torque** 128lb ft (17.7kgm) at 3000rpm (130lb ft (18kgm) at 3000rpm from Nov 1979) **Transmission** Four-speed manual gearbox (1978-83), five-speed manual gearbox (1983-86), optional Ford C3 three-speed automatic **Gear ratios** 4th 1.00, 3rd 1.37, 2nd 1.97, 1st 3.65, rev 3.16; 1983-86: 5th 0.825, 4th 1.00, 3rd 1.37, 2nd 1.97, 1st 3.65, rev 3.16 **Final drive** 3.220 **Top gear speed per 1000rpm** 19.9mph (32.0kmh), or 20.8mph (33.4kmh) from 1983 **Top speed** 112mph (180kmh), 113mph (183kmh) from Nov 1979 **0–100kmh** 12.0 secs 13.0 secs with automatic)

3000 (1978–81) As 3000 (UK)

3000 X-Pack (1978–80) As 3000 X-Pack (UK) except: **Fuel system** One single-choke carburettor

2.8i (1981–84) As 2.8i (UK)

2.8 Turbo (1981–82) As 2.8i (UK) except: **Engine** Fitted with Garrett AiResearch turbocharger **Fuel system** Single Solex 38/38 EEIT twin-choke carburettor **Maximum power** 188bhp at 5500rpm **Maximum torque** 194lb ft (26.8kgm) at 4500rpm **Wheels/tyres** 6.5 × 13in or 7.5 × 14in alloy wheels with 235/60 13 or 250/60 14 tyres **Width** 73in (1854mm) **Unladen weight** 2756lb (1250kg) **Top speed** 137mph (220kmh) **0–100kmh** 8.0 secs

ACKNOWLEDGEMENTS

On the awkward subject of Capri production figures, many thanks
are due to David Burgess-Wise, Ken Bandy at Ford Supply
Manufacturing and Marie at the National Motor Museum Library at
Beaulieu. Most of the photographs used come from Ford's
photographic archive, as researched by Ed Herridge, and also from
David Hodges, the Bay View Books archive and the author's own
collection. Thanks to Jim Lim Bim Sim for CD-ROMming.

**The very last Capri, a 280, was built on 19 December
1986 at the Cologne plant. The white letters say that
1,886,647 Capris were made in total, but current
research has revised that figure to 1,922,847.**